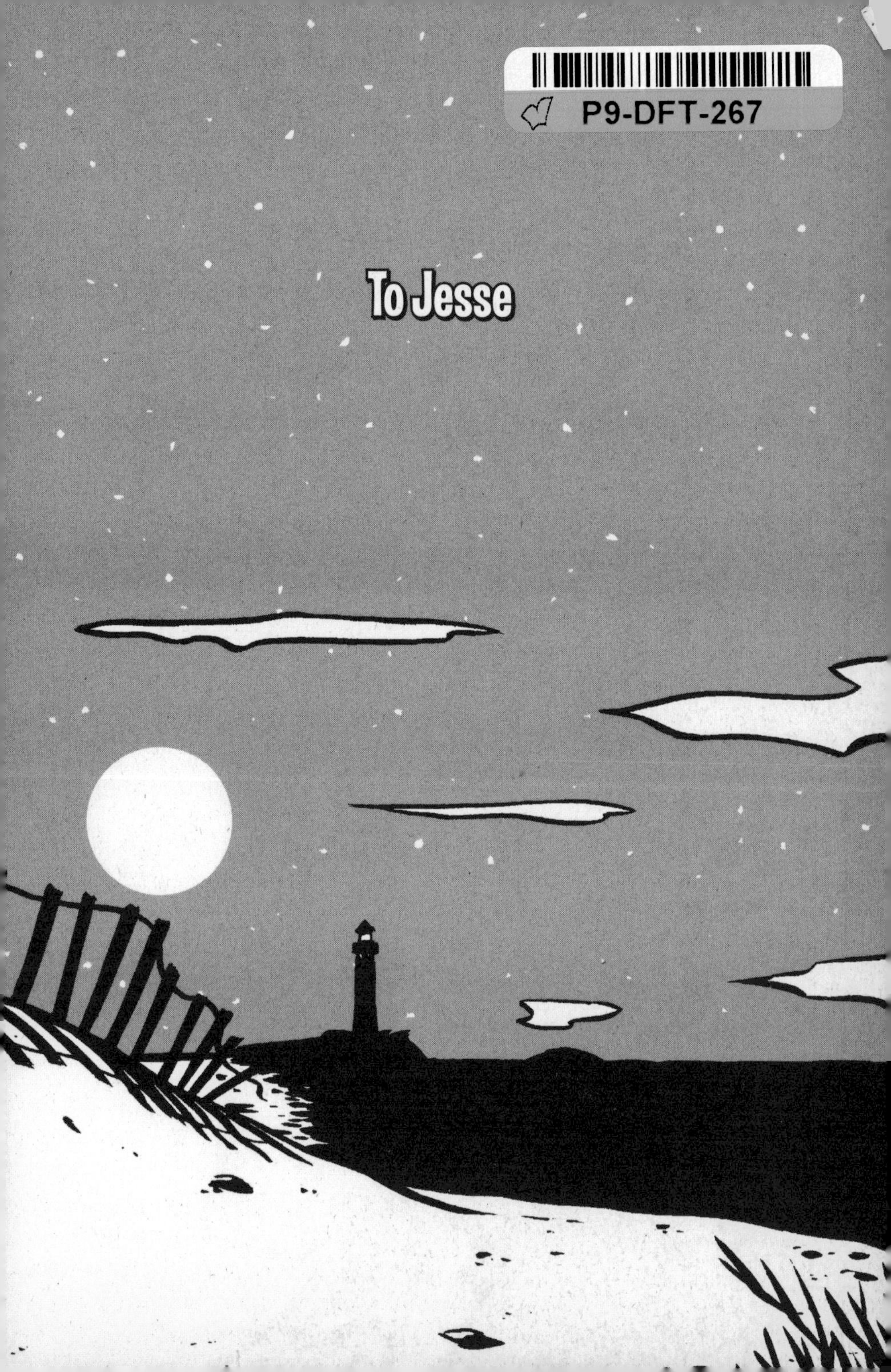

To Jesse

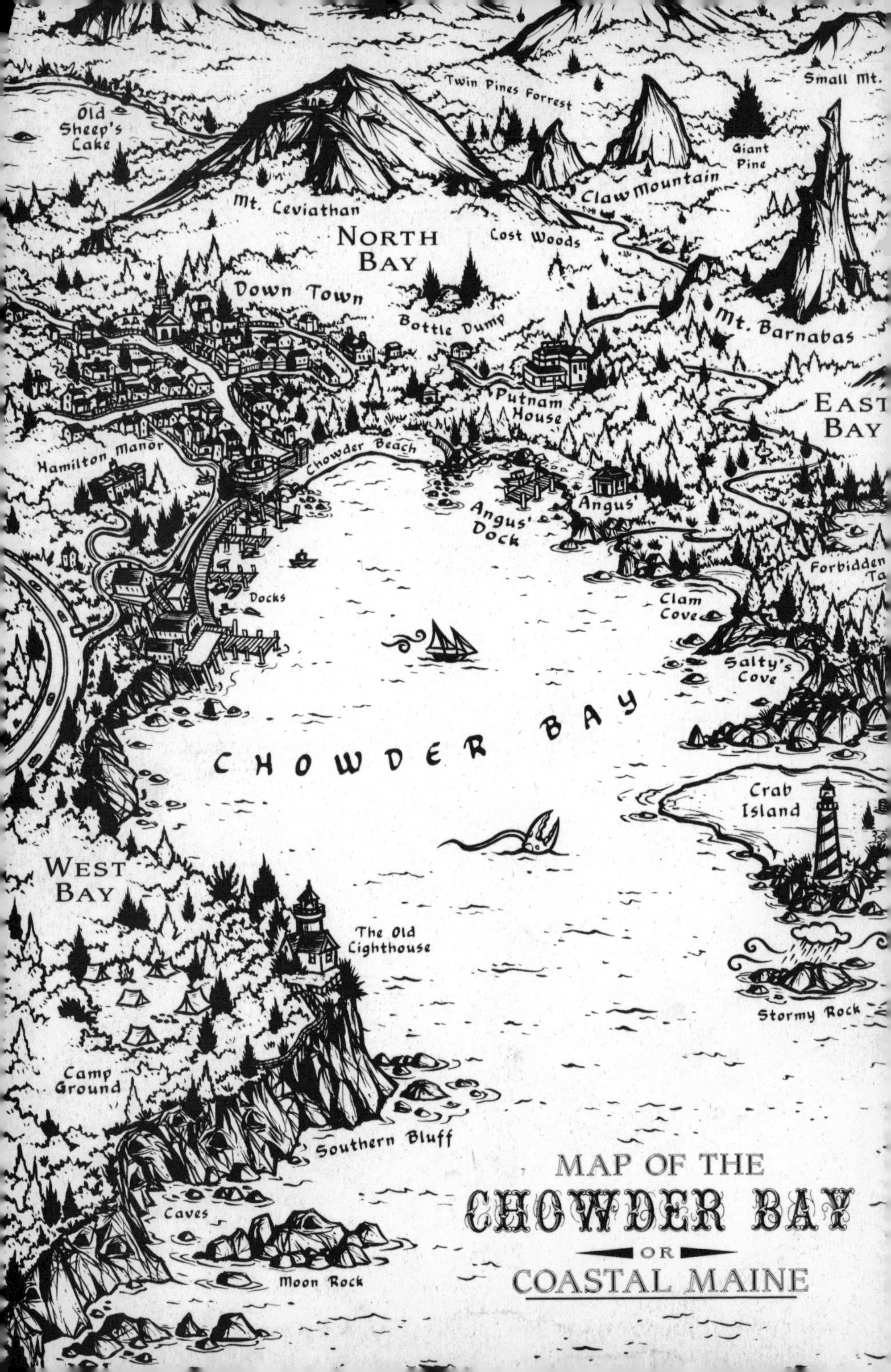

Old Sheep's Lake
Twin Pines Forrest
Small Mt.
Giant Pine
Claw Mountain
Mt. Leviathan
North Bay
Lost Woods
Down Town
Bottle Dump
Mt. Barnabas
East Bay
Putnam House
Hamilton Manor
Chowder Beach
Angus'
Angus' Dock
Docks
Forbidden
Clam Cove
Salty's Cove
Chowder Bay
Crab Island
West Bay
The Old Lighthouse
Stormy Rock
Camp Ground
Southern Bluff
Caves
Moon Rock
MAP OF THE
CHOWDER BAY
OR
COASTAL MAINE

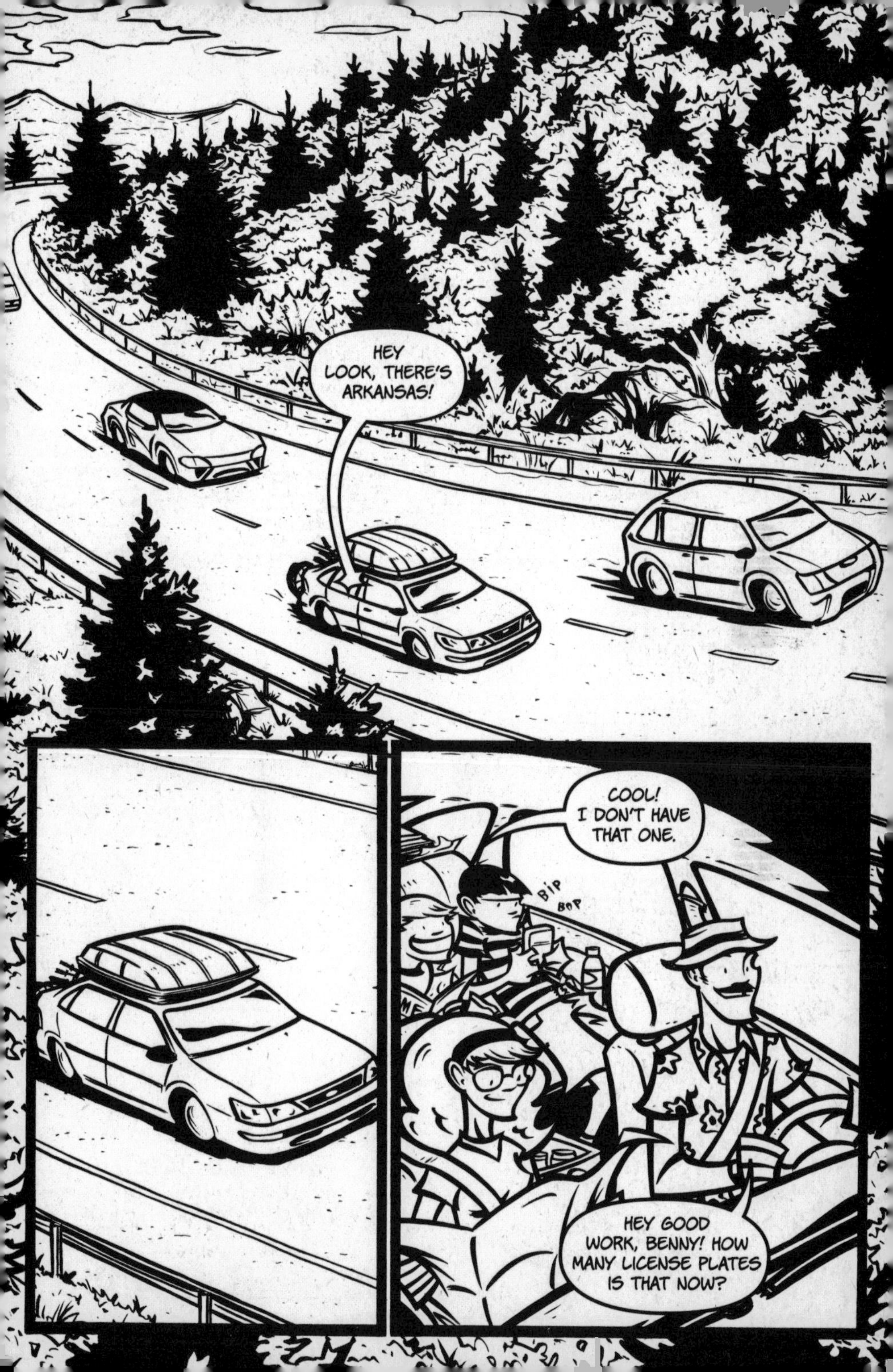
HEY LOOK, THERE'S ARKANSAS!
COOL! I DON'T HAVE THAT ONE.
BIP BOP
HEY GOOD WORK, BENNY! HOW MANY LICENSE PLATES IS THAT NOW?

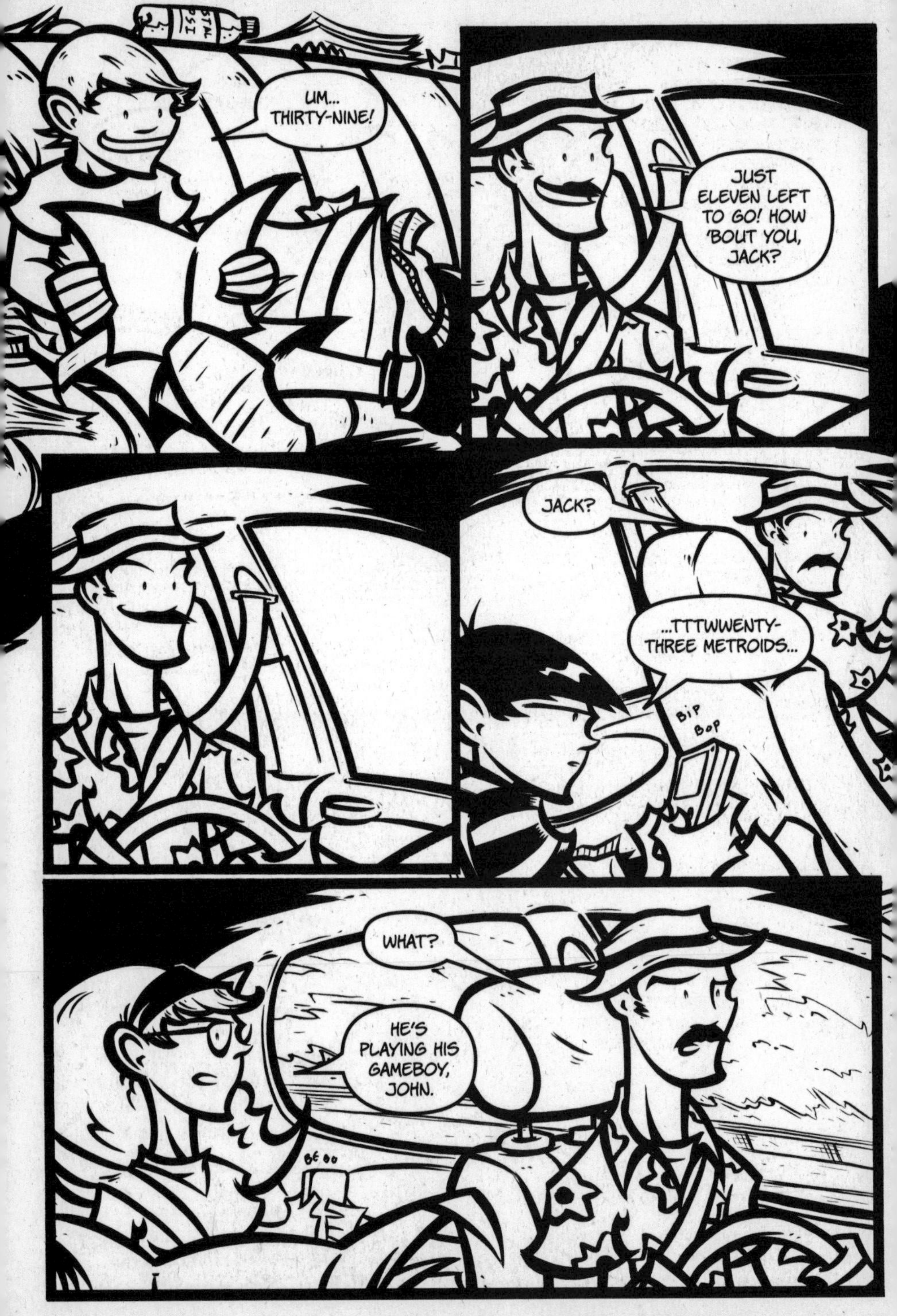
UM... THIRTY-NINE!
JUST ELEVEN LEFT TO GO! HOW 'BOUT YOU, JACK?
JACK?
...TTTWWENTY-THREE METROIDS...
BIP BOP
WHAT?
HE'S PLAYING HIS GAMEBOY, JOHN.

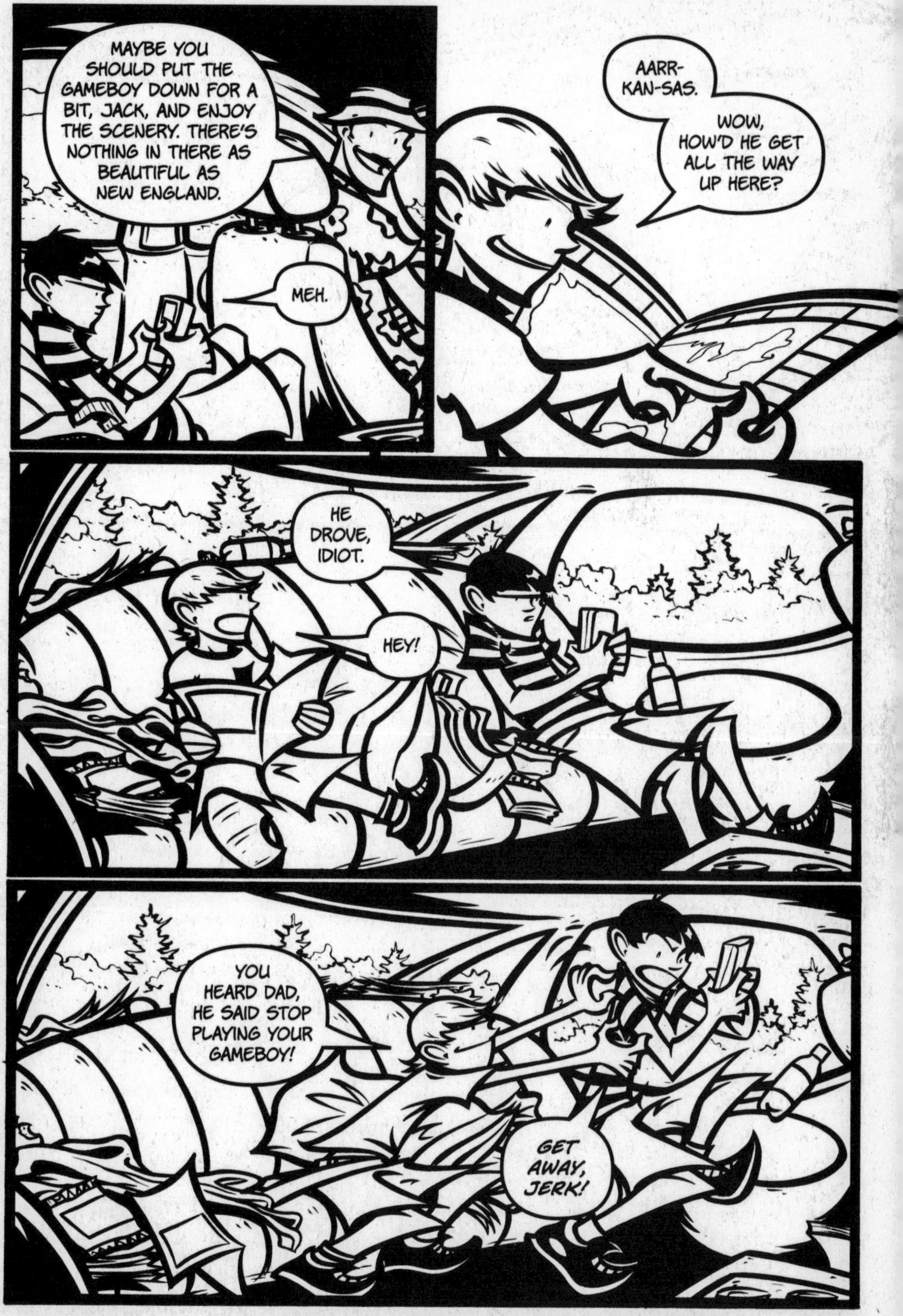
MAYBE YOU SHOULD PUT THE GAMEBOY DOWN FOR A BIT, JACK, AND ENJOY THE SCENERY. THERE'S NOTHING IN THERE AS BEAUTIFUL AS NEW ENGLAND.
MEH.
AARR-KAN-SAS.
WOW, HOW'D HE GET ALL THE WAY UP HERE?
HE DROVE, IDIOT.
HEY!
YOU HEARD DAD, HE SAID STOP PLAYING YOUR GAMEBOY!
GET AWAY, JERK!

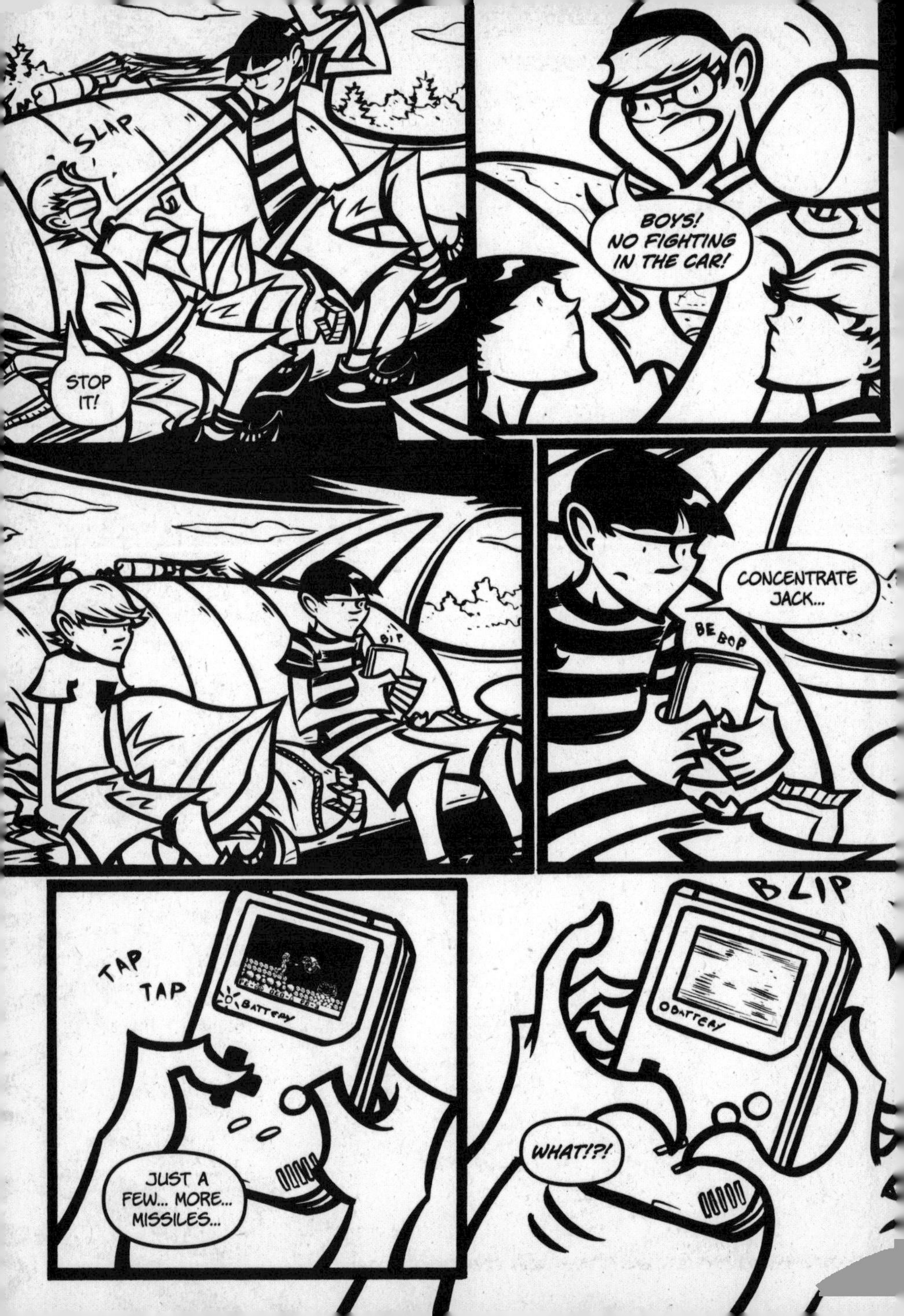
SLAP
STOP IT!
BOYS! NO FIGHTING IN THE CAR!
BIP
CONCENTRATE JACK...
BE BOP
TAP
TAP
BATTERY
JUST A FEW... MORE... MISSILES...
BLIP
BATTERY
WHAT!?!

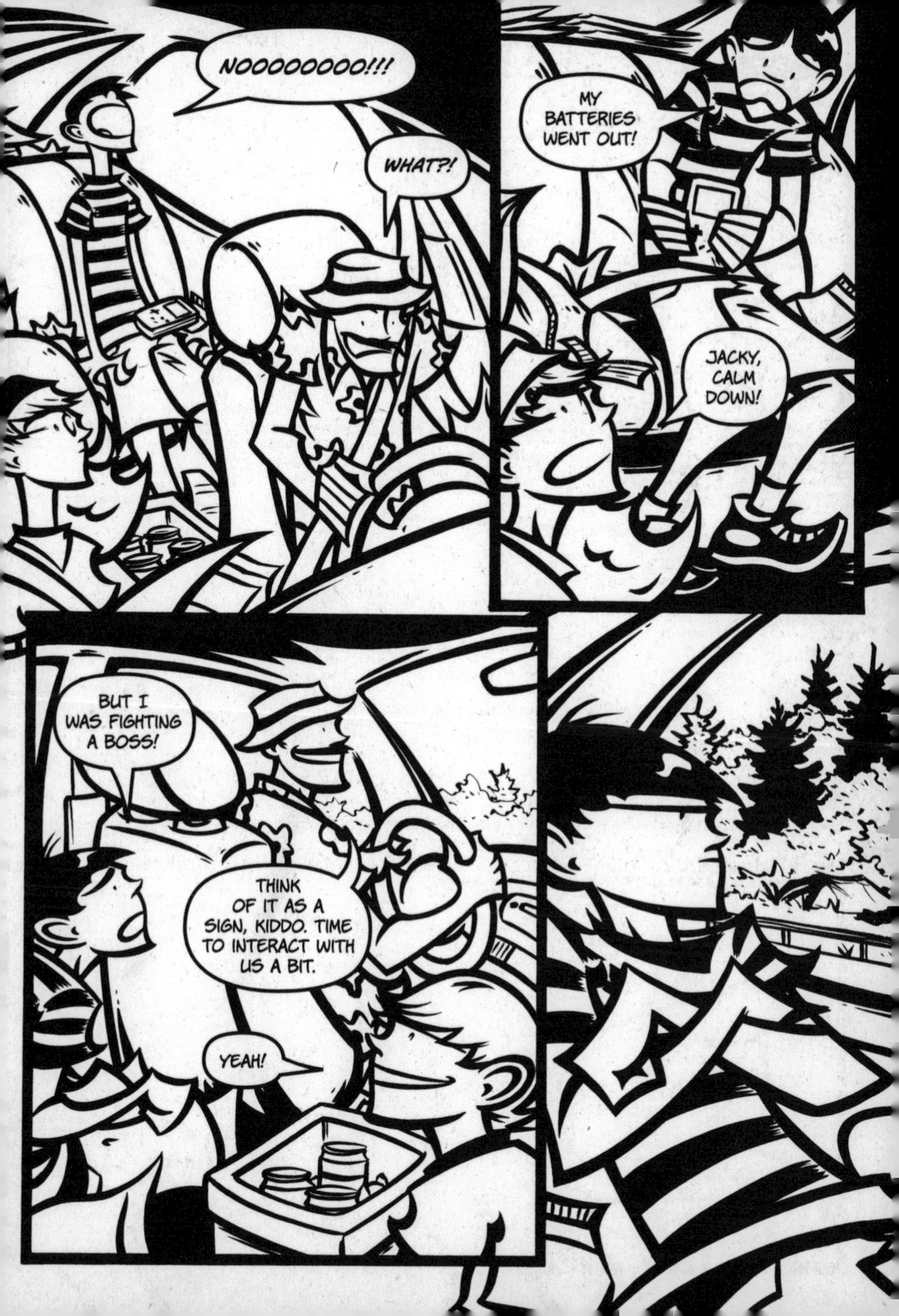
NOOOOOOOO!!!
WHAT?!
MY BATTERIES WENT OUT!
JACKY, CALM DOWN!
BUT I WAS FIGHTING A BOSS!
THINK OF IT AS A SIGN, KIDDO. TIME TO INTERACT WITH US A BIT.
YEAH!

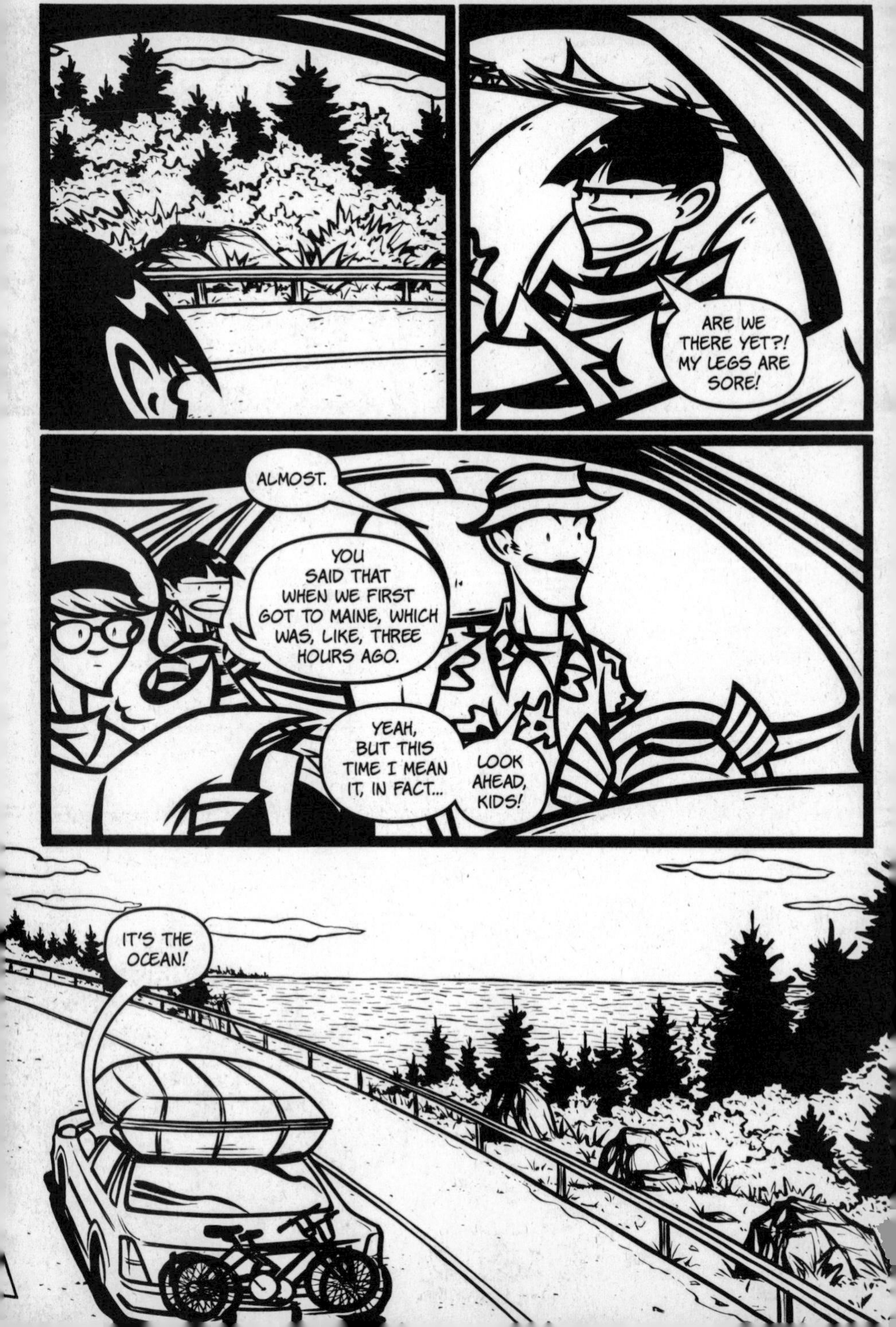
ARE WE THERE YET?! MY LEGS ARE SORE!
ALMOST.
YOU SAID THAT WHEN WE FIRST GOT TO MAINE, WHICH WAS, LIKE, THREE HOURS AGO.
YEAH, BUT THIS TIME I MEAN IT, IN FACT...
LOOK AHEAD, KIDS!
IT'S THE OCEAN!

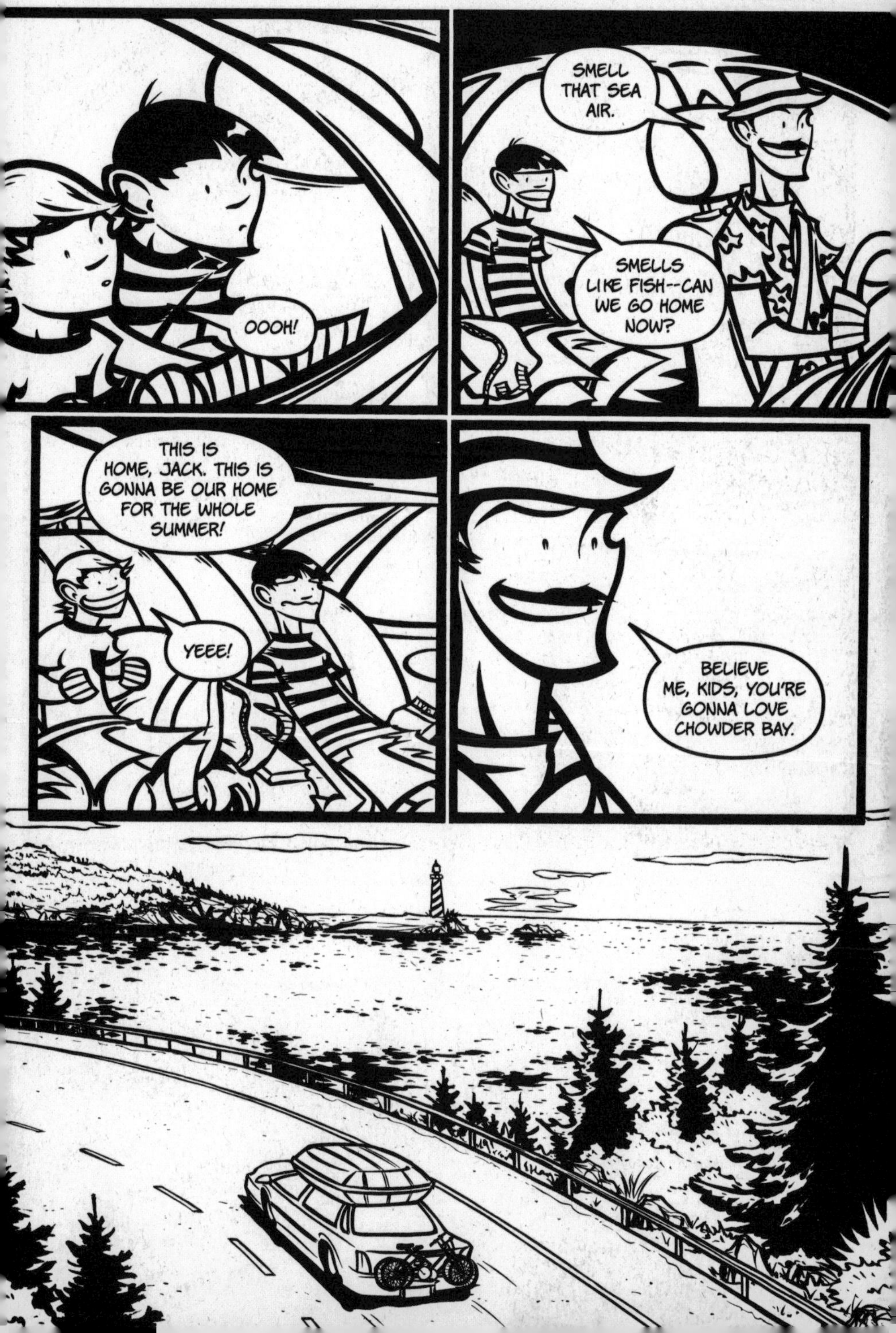
OOOH!
SMELL THAT SEA AIR.
SMELLS LIKE FISH--CAN WE GO HOME NOW?
THIS IS HOME, JACK. THIS IS GONNA BE OUR HOME FOR THE WHOLE SUMMER!
YEEE!
BELIEVE ME, KIDS, YOU'RE GONNA LOVE CHOWDER BAY.

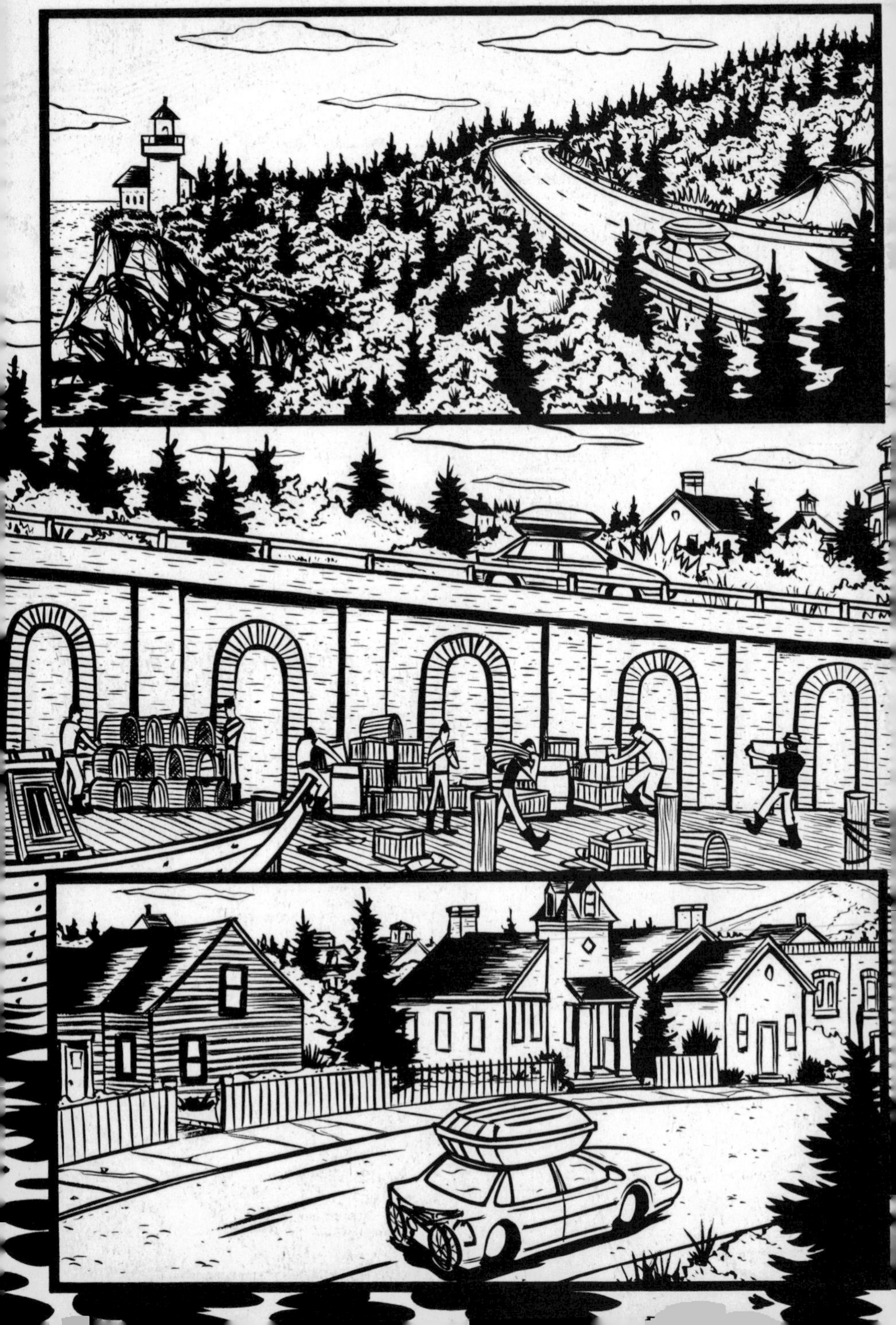

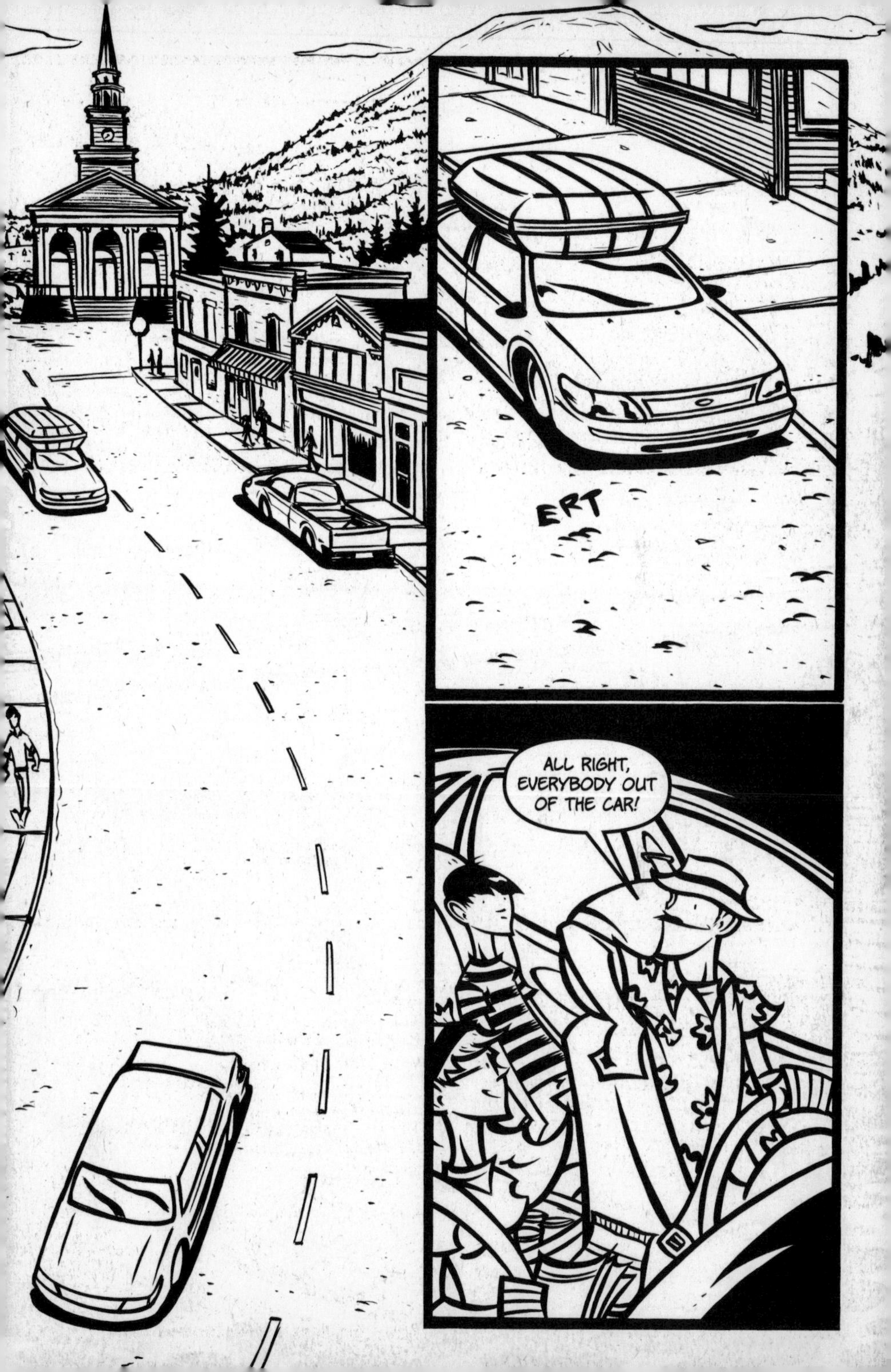
ERT
ALL RIGHT, EVERYBODY OUT OF THE CAR!

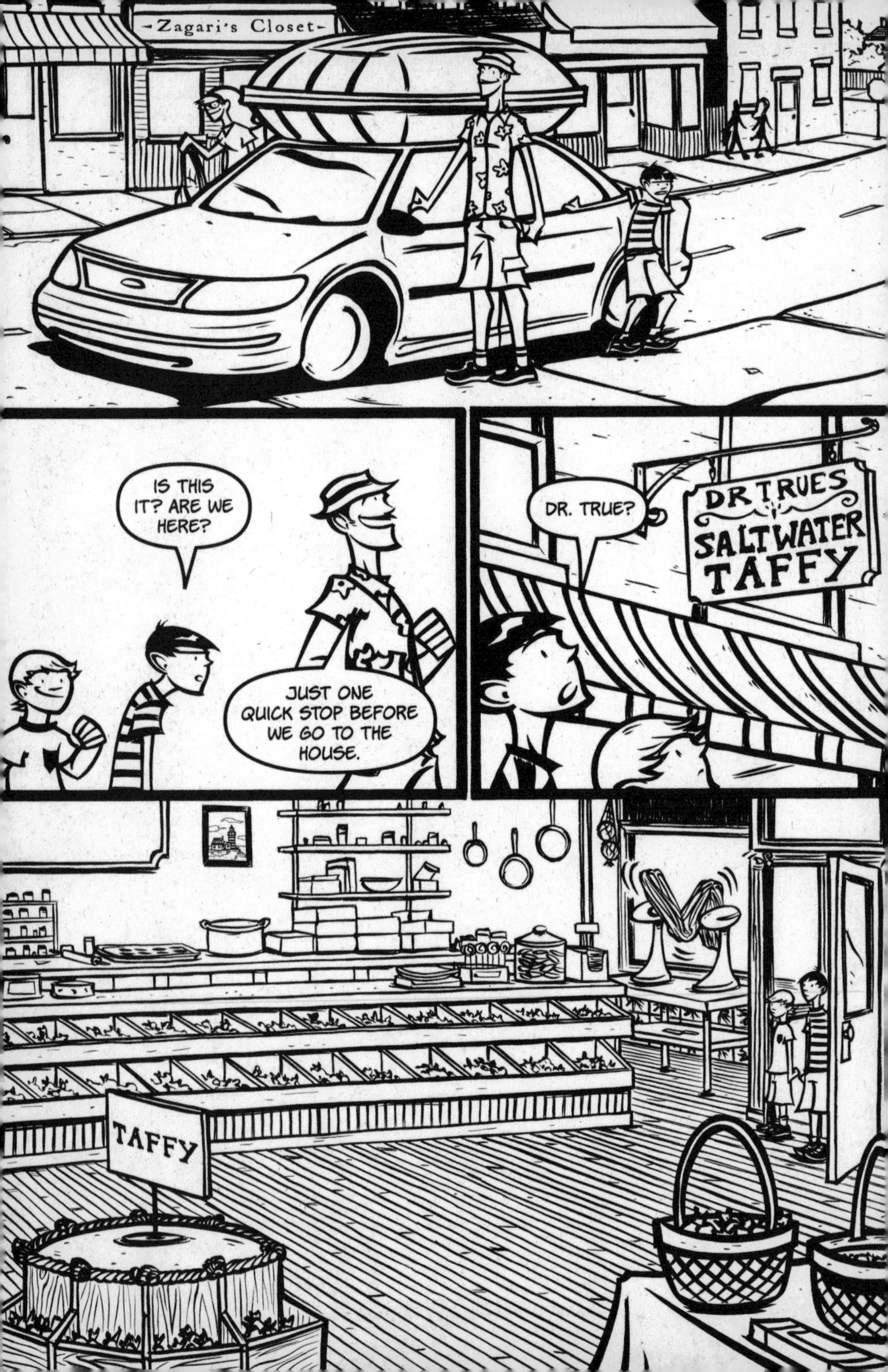

Zagari's Closet
IS THIS IT? ARE WE HERE?
JUST ONE QUICK STOP BEFORE WE GO TO THE HOUSE.
DR. TRUE?
DR TRUES SALTWATER TAFFY
TAFFY

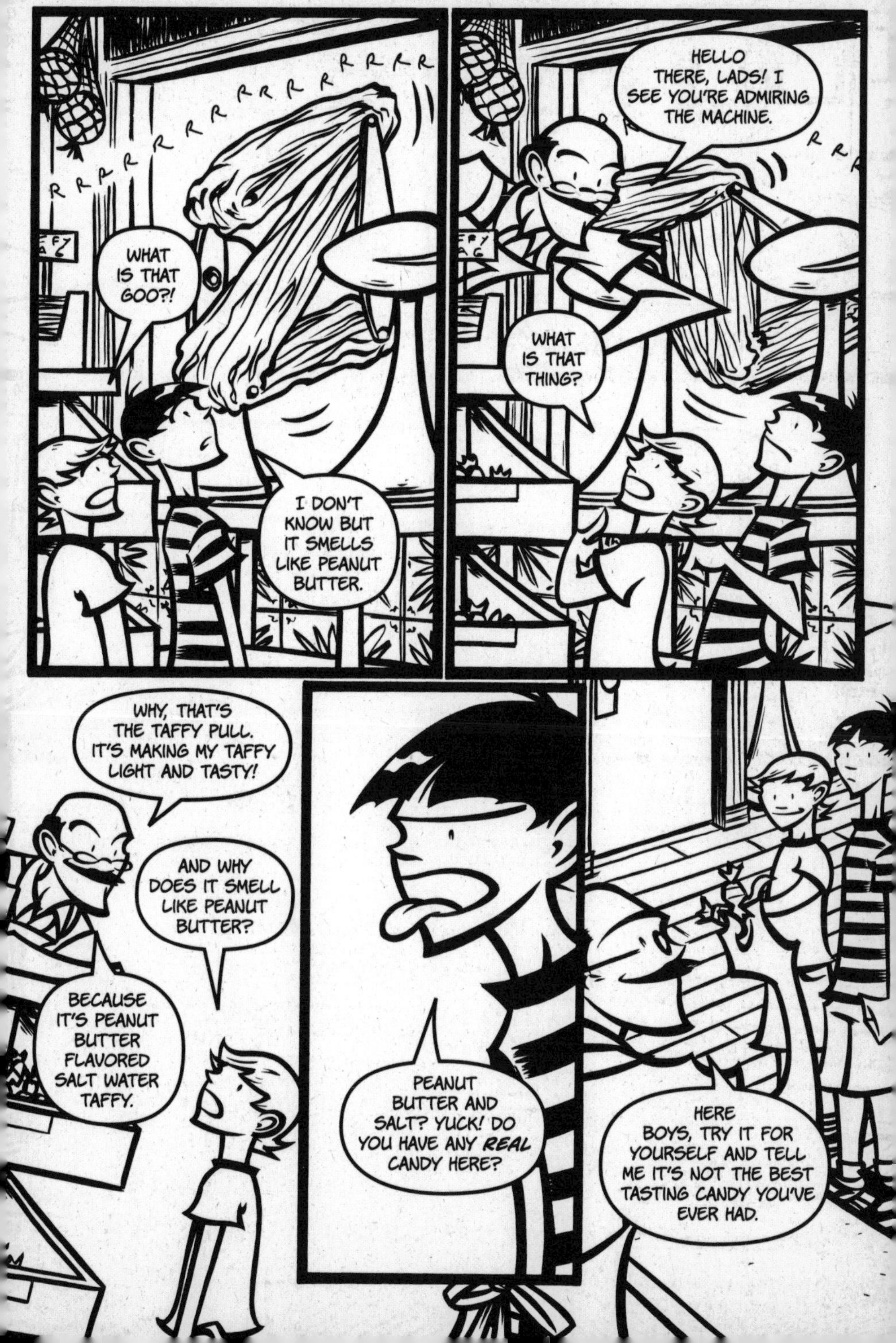
RRRRRRRRRRRRRRRRRRRRRRR
WHAT IS THAT GOO?!
I DON'T KNOW BUT IT SMELLS LIKE PEANUT BUTTER.
HELLO THERE, LADS! I SEE YOU'RE ADMIRING THE MACHINE.
WHAT IS THAT THING?
WHY, THAT'S THE TAFFY PULL. IT'S MAKING MY TAFFY LIGHT AND TASTY!
AND WHY DOES IT SMELL LIKE PEANUT BUTTER?
BECAUSE IT'S PEANUT BUTTER FLAVORED SALT WATER TAFFY.
PEANUT BUTTER AND SALT? YUCK! DO YOU HAVE ANY *REAL* CANDY HERE?
HERE BOYS, TRY IT FOR YOURSELF AND TELL ME IT'S NOT THE BEST TASTING CANDY YOU'VE EVER HAD.

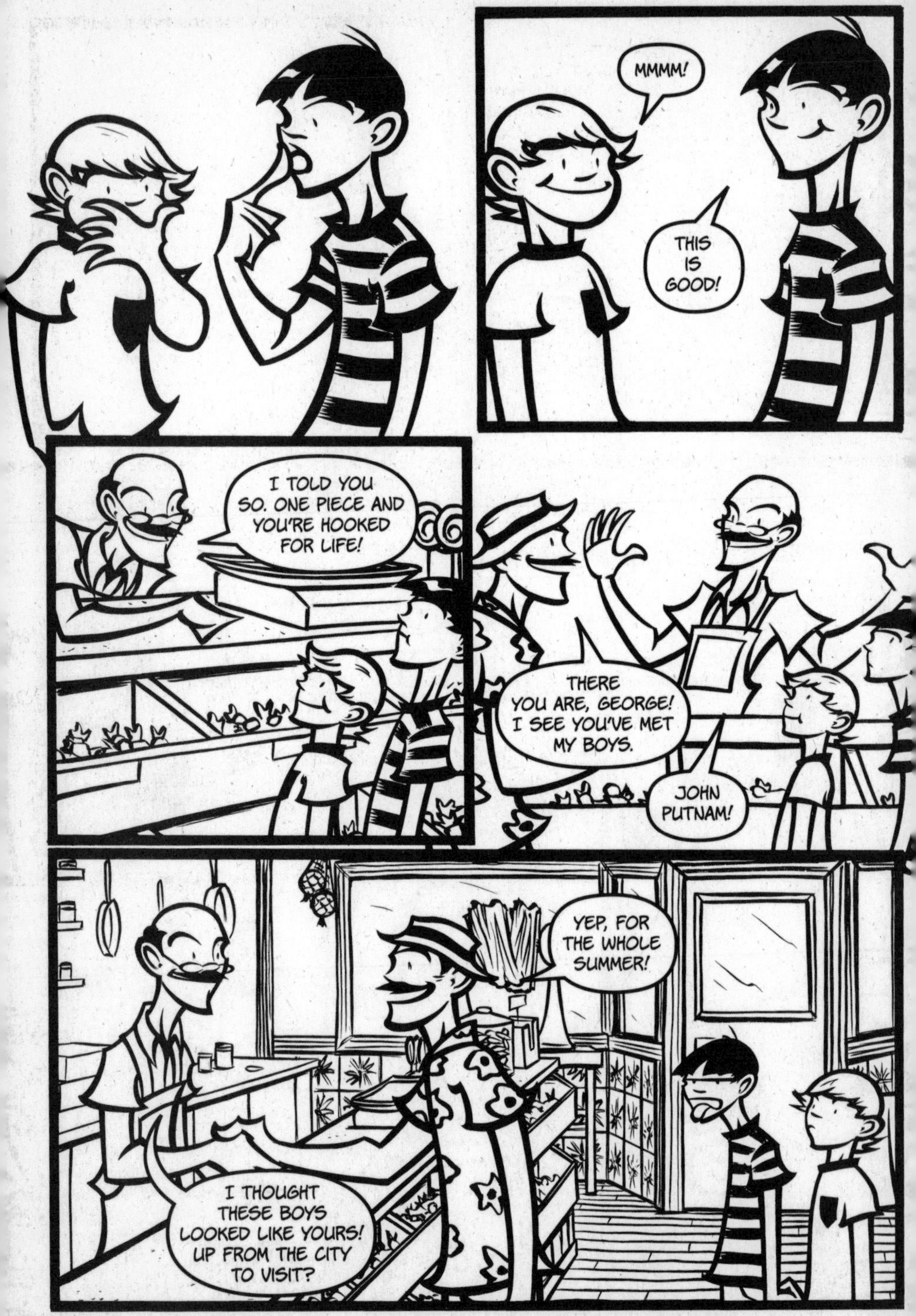
MMMM!
THIS IS GOOD!
I TOLD YOU SO. ONE PIECE AND YOU'RE HOOKED FOR LIFE!
THERE YOU ARE, GEORGE! I SEE YOU'VE MET MY BOYS.
JOHN PUTNAM!
YEP, FOR THE WHOLE SUMMER!
I THOUGHT THESE BOYS LOOKED LIKE YOURS! UP FROM THE CITY TO VISIT?

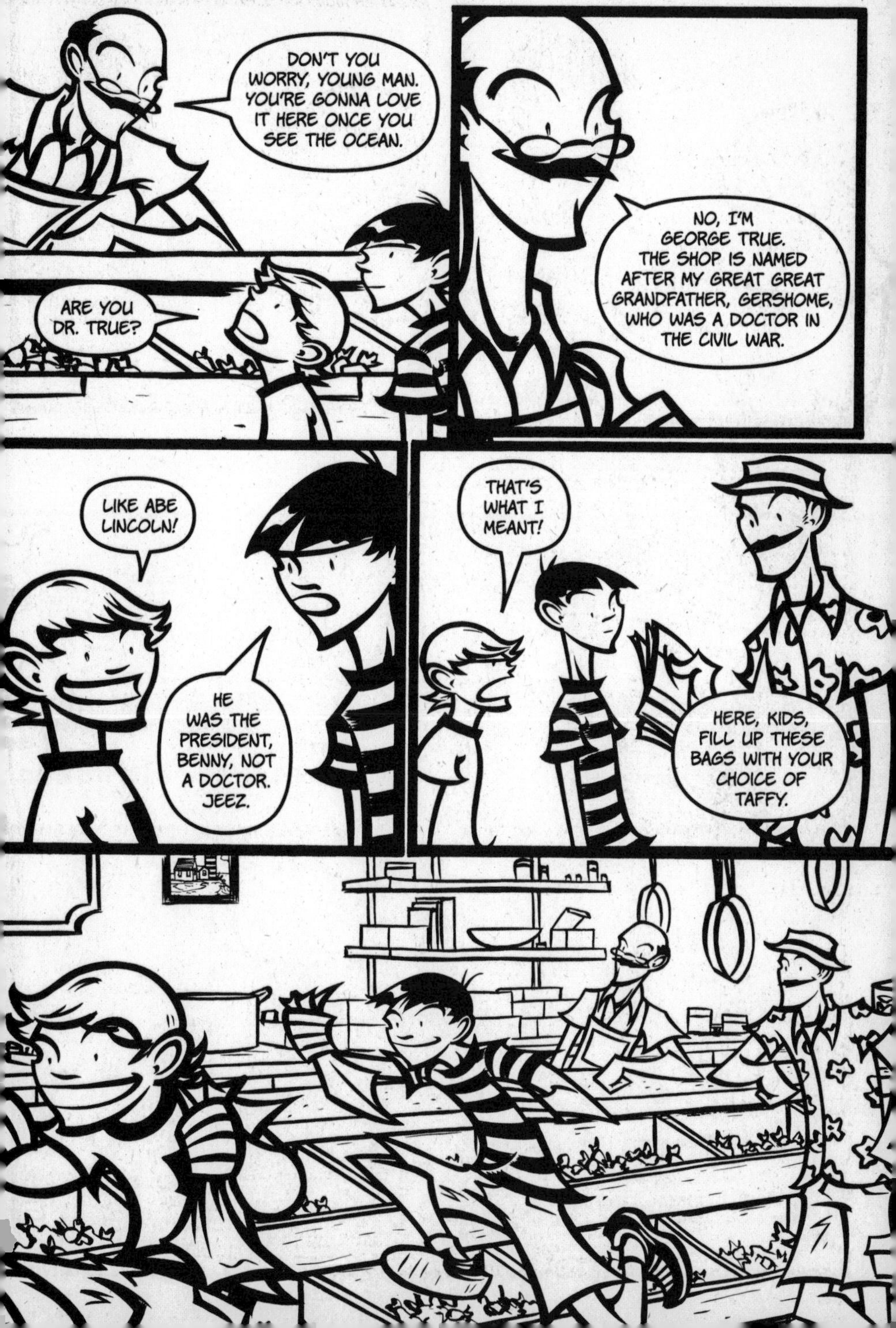
DON'T YOU WORRY, YOUNG MAN. YOU'RE GONNA LOVE IT HERE ONCE YOU SEE THE OCEAN.
ARE YOU DR. TRUE?
NO, I'M GEORGE TRUE. THE SHOP IS NAMED AFTER MY GREAT GREAT GRANDFATHER, GERSHOME, WHO WAS A DOCTOR IN THE CIVIL WAR.
LIKE ABE LINCOLN!
HE WAS THE PRESIDENT, BENNY, NOT A DOCTOR. JEEZ.
THAT'S WHAT I MEANT!
HERE, KIDS, FILL UP THESE BAGS WITH YOUR CHOICE OF TAFFY.

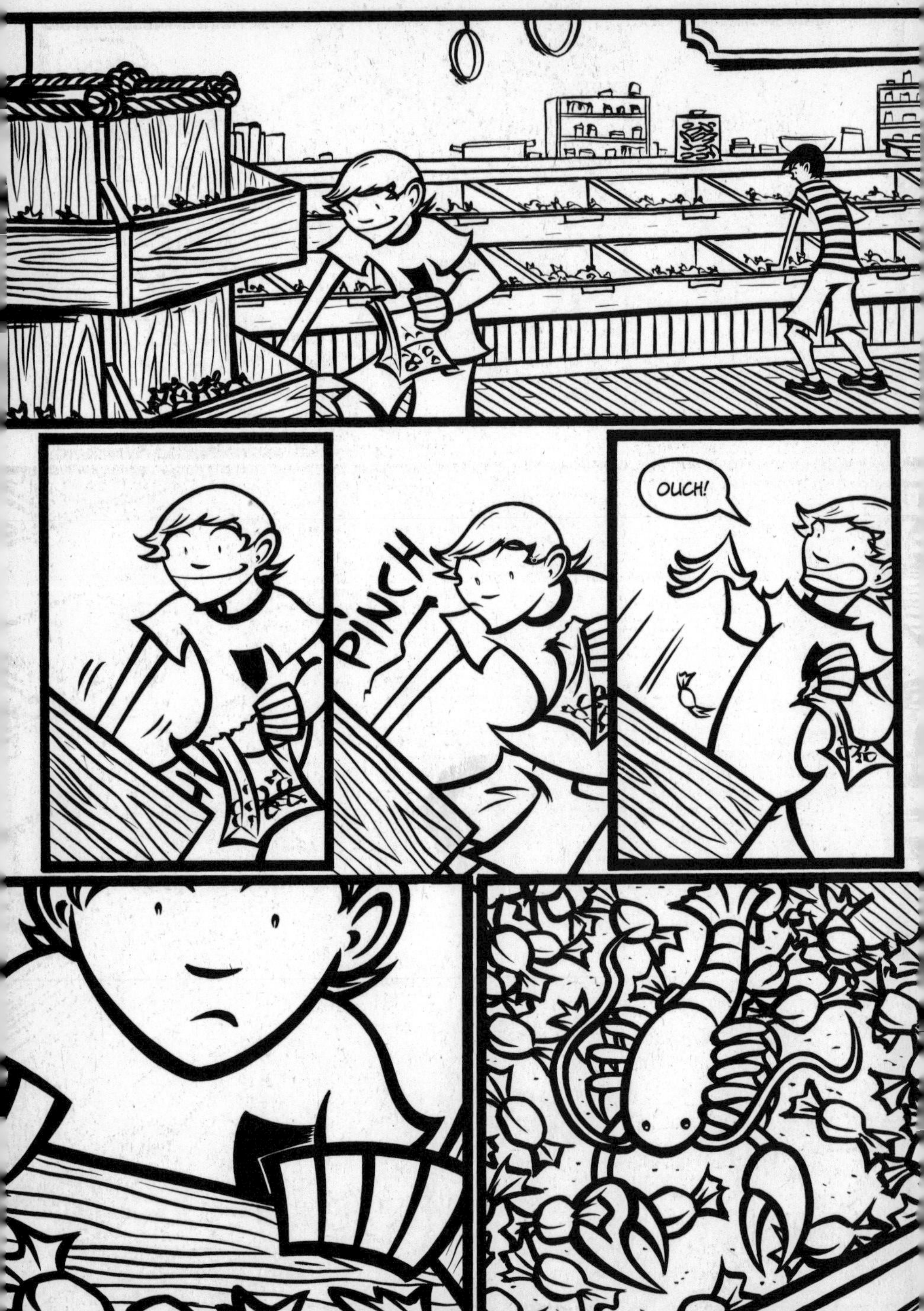

PINCH
OUCH!

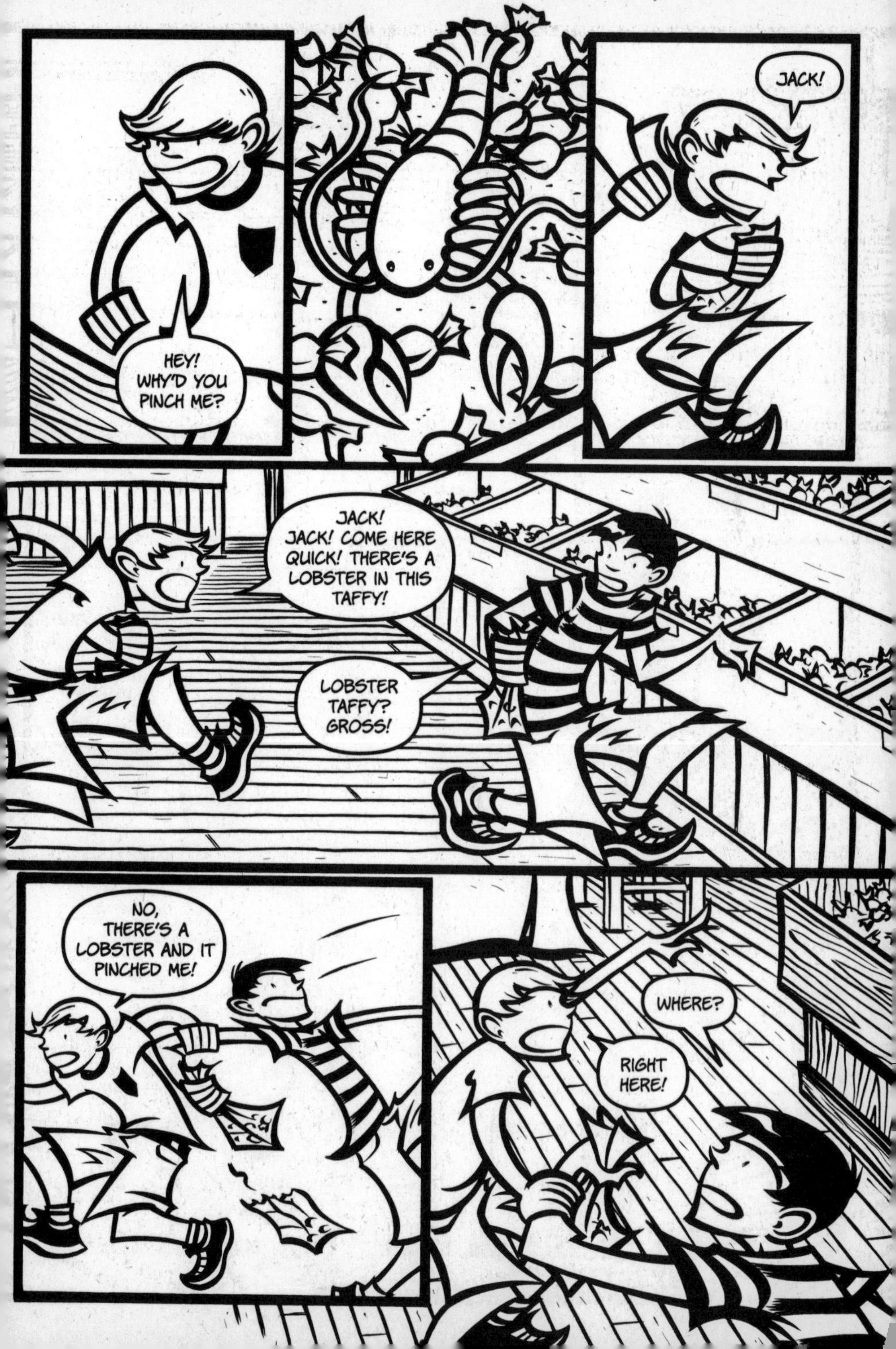
HEY! WHY'D YOU PINCH ME?
JACK!
JACK! JACK! COME HERE QUICK! THERE'S A LOBSTER IN THIS TAFFY!
LOBSTER TAFFY? GROSS!
NO, THERE'S A LOBSTER AND IT PINCHED ME!
WHERE?
RIGHT HERE!

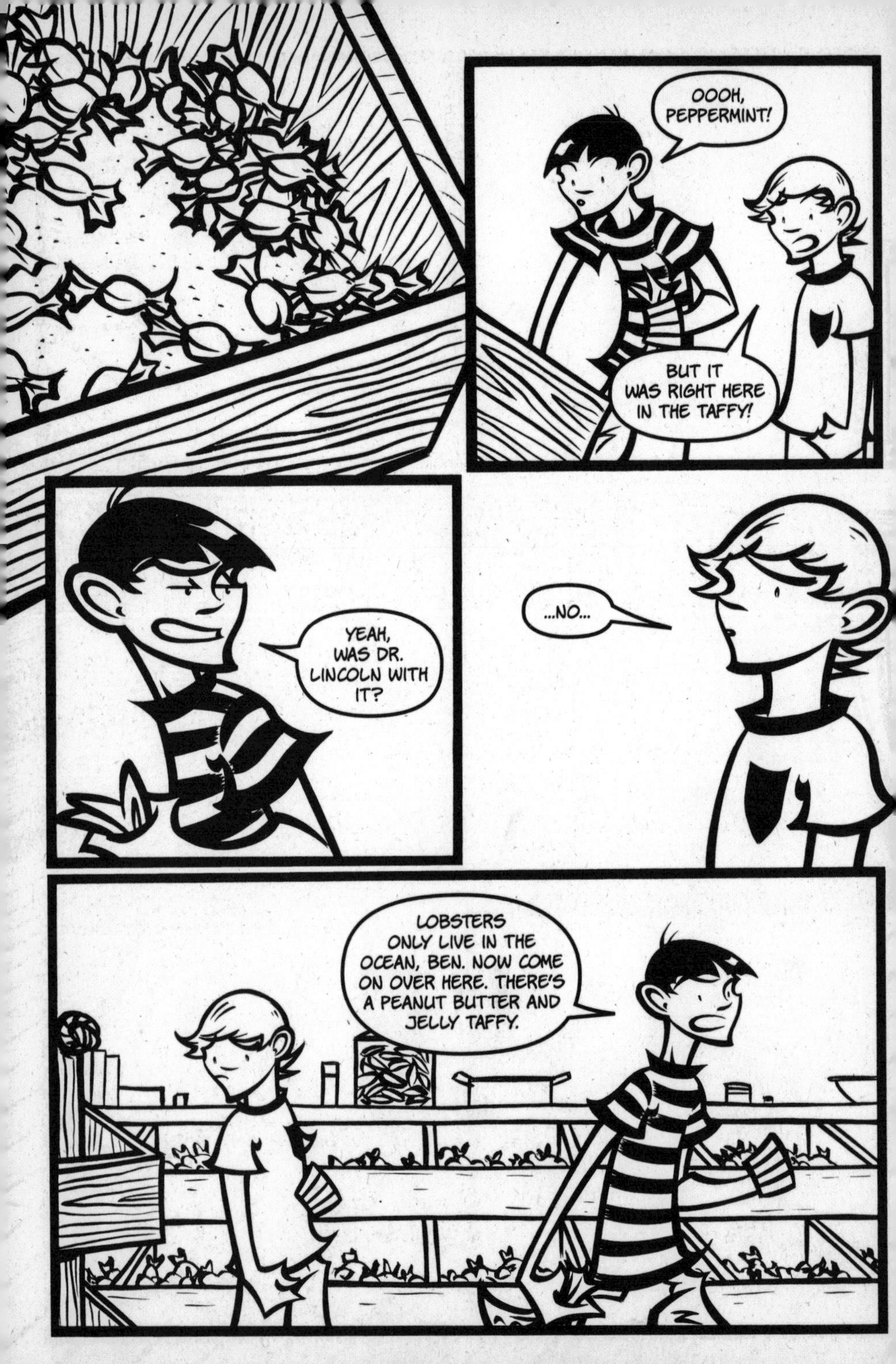
OOOH, PEPPERMINT!
BUT IT WAS RIGHT HERE IN THE TAFFY!
YEAH, WAS DR. LINCOLN WITH IT?
...NO...
LOBSTERS ONLY LIVE IN THE OCEAN, BEN. NOW COME ON OVER HERE. THERE'S A PEANUT BUTTER AND JELLY TAFFY.

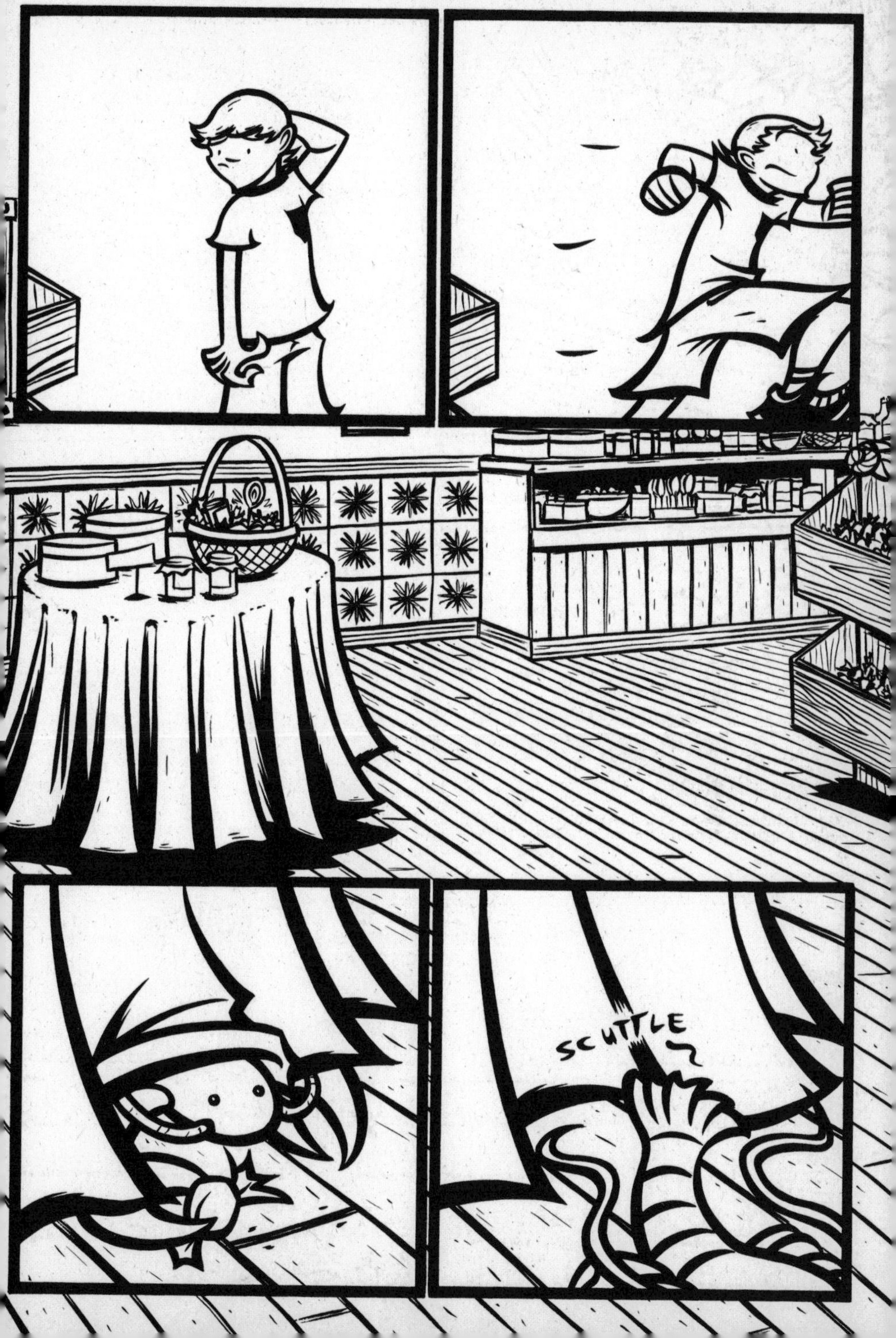
SCUTTLE

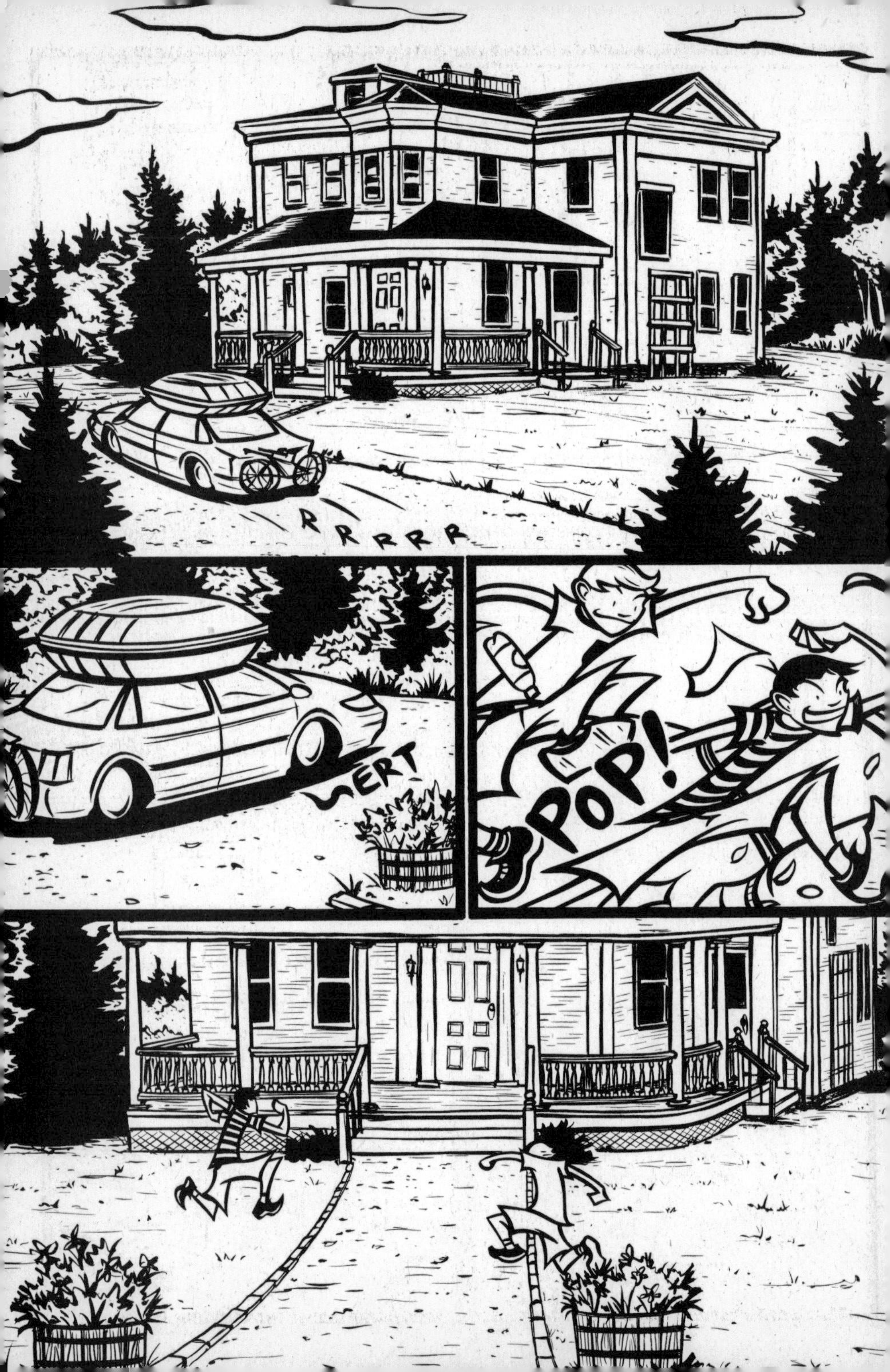
RRRRR
VERT
POP!

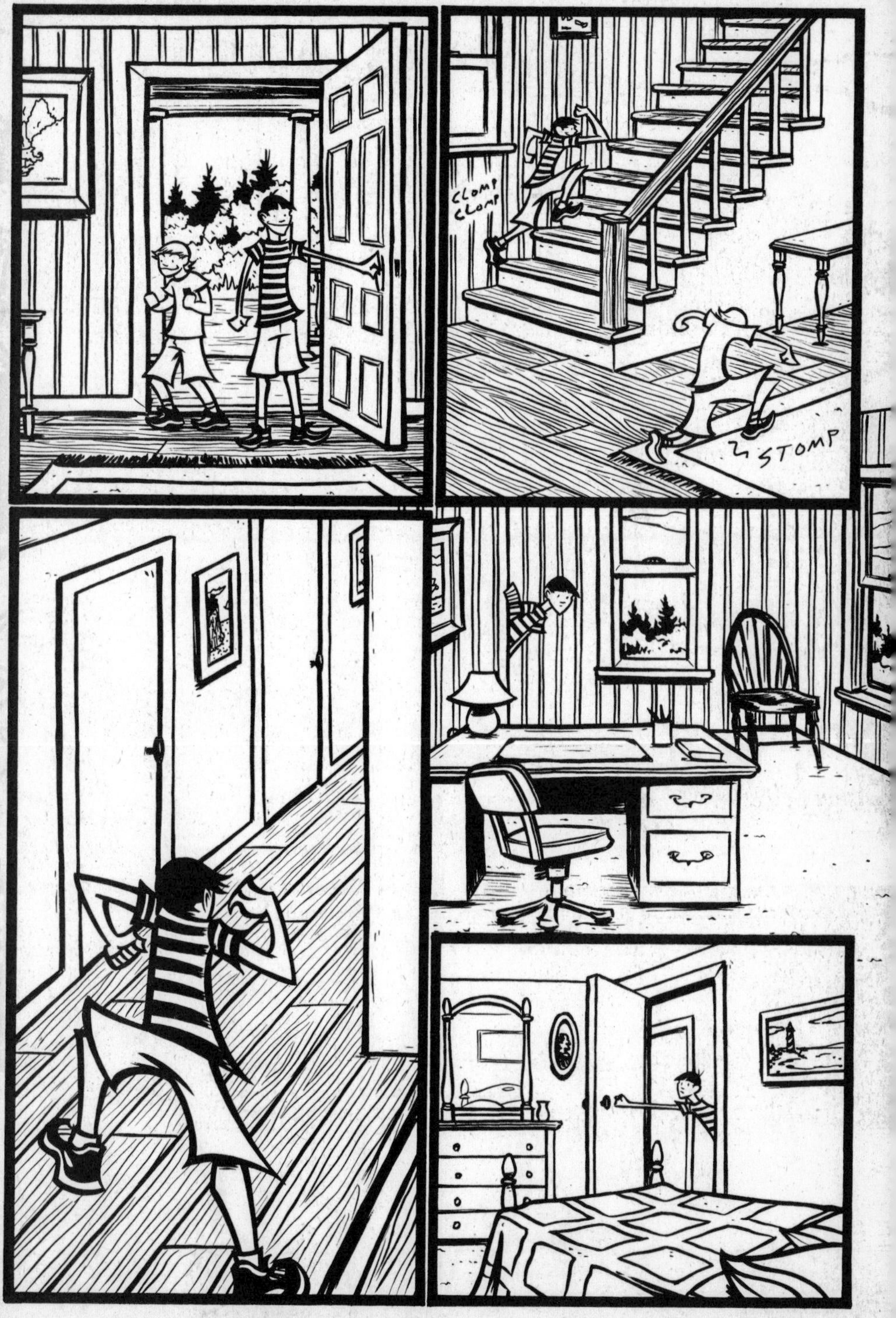
CLOMP
CLOMP
STOMP

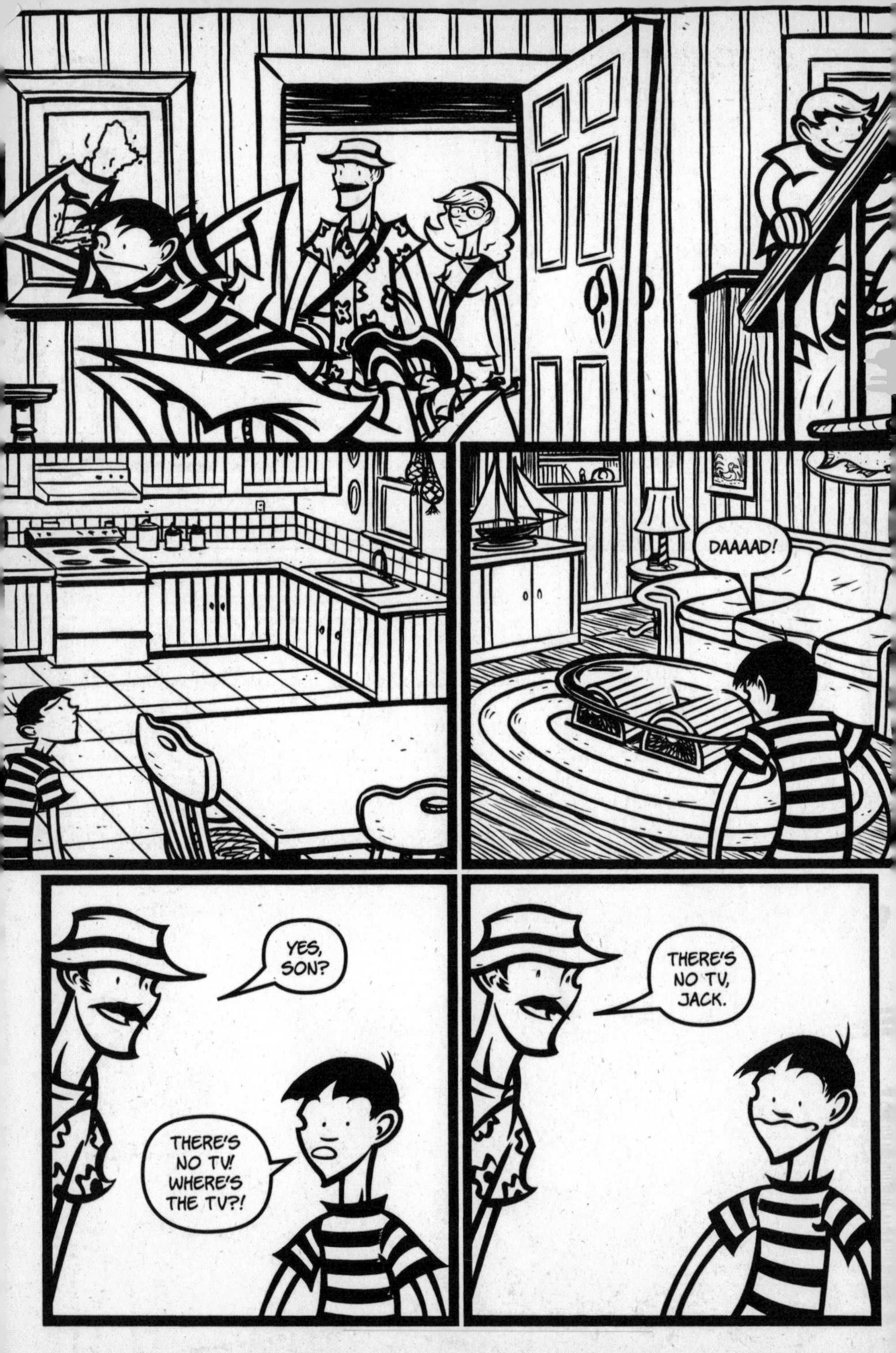
DAAAAD!
YES, SON?
THERE'S NO TV! WHERE'S THE TV?!
THERE'S NO TV, JACK.

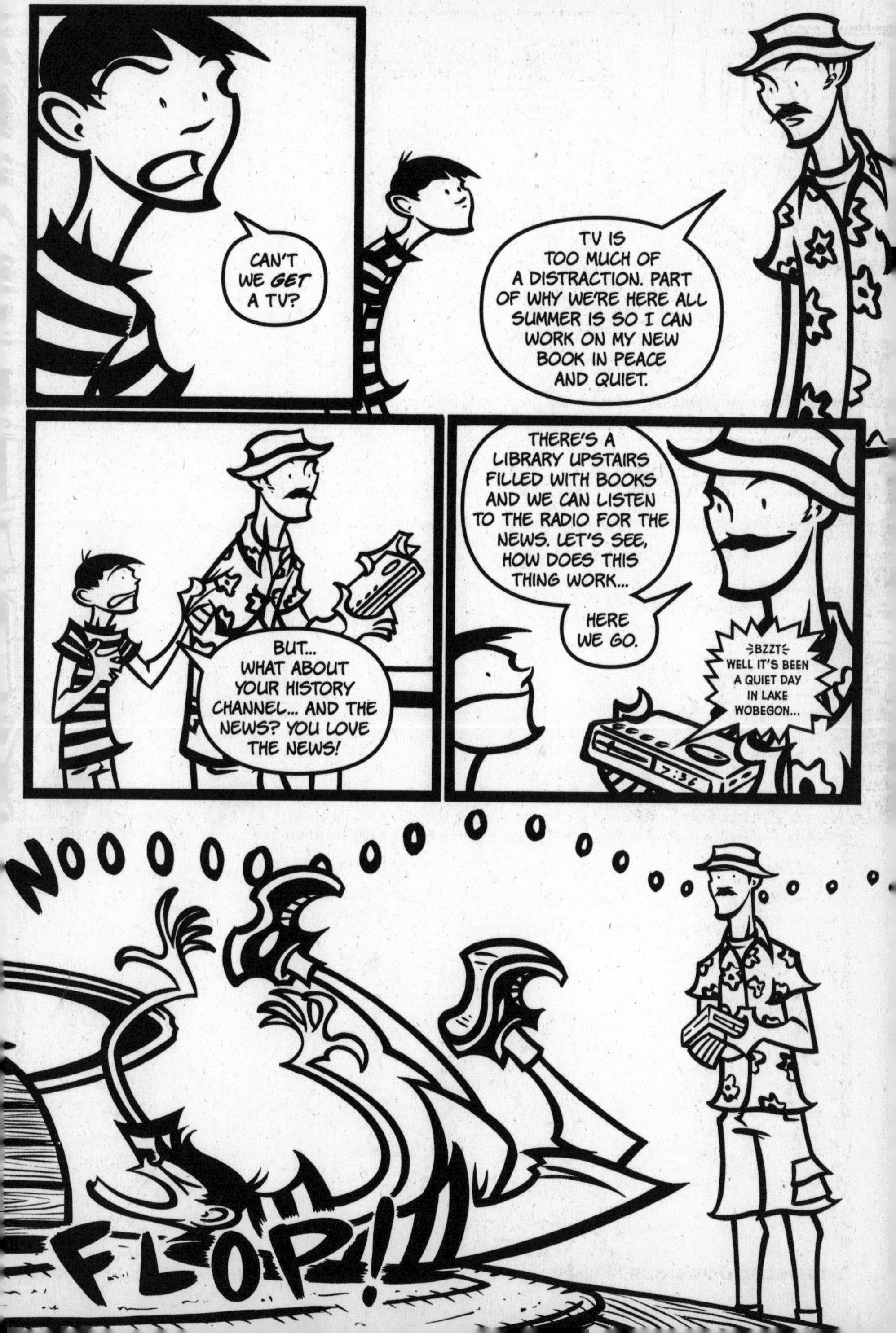
CAN'T WE *GET* A TV?
TV IS TOO MUCH OF A DISTRACTION. PART OF WHY WE'RE HERE ALL SUMMER IS SO I CAN WORK ON MY NEW BOOK IN PEACE AND QUIET.
BUT... WHAT ABOUT YOUR HISTORY CHANNEL... AND THE NEWS? YOU LOVE THE NEWS!
THERE'S A LIBRARY UPSTAIRS FILLED WITH BOOKS AND WE CAN LISTEN TO THE RADIO FOR THE NEWS. LET'S SEE, HOW DOES THIS THING WORK...
HERE WE GO.
BZZT WELL IT'S BEEN A QUIET DAY IN LAKE WOBEGON...
7:36
NOOOOOOOOOOOOOOOOOOO...
FLOP!!

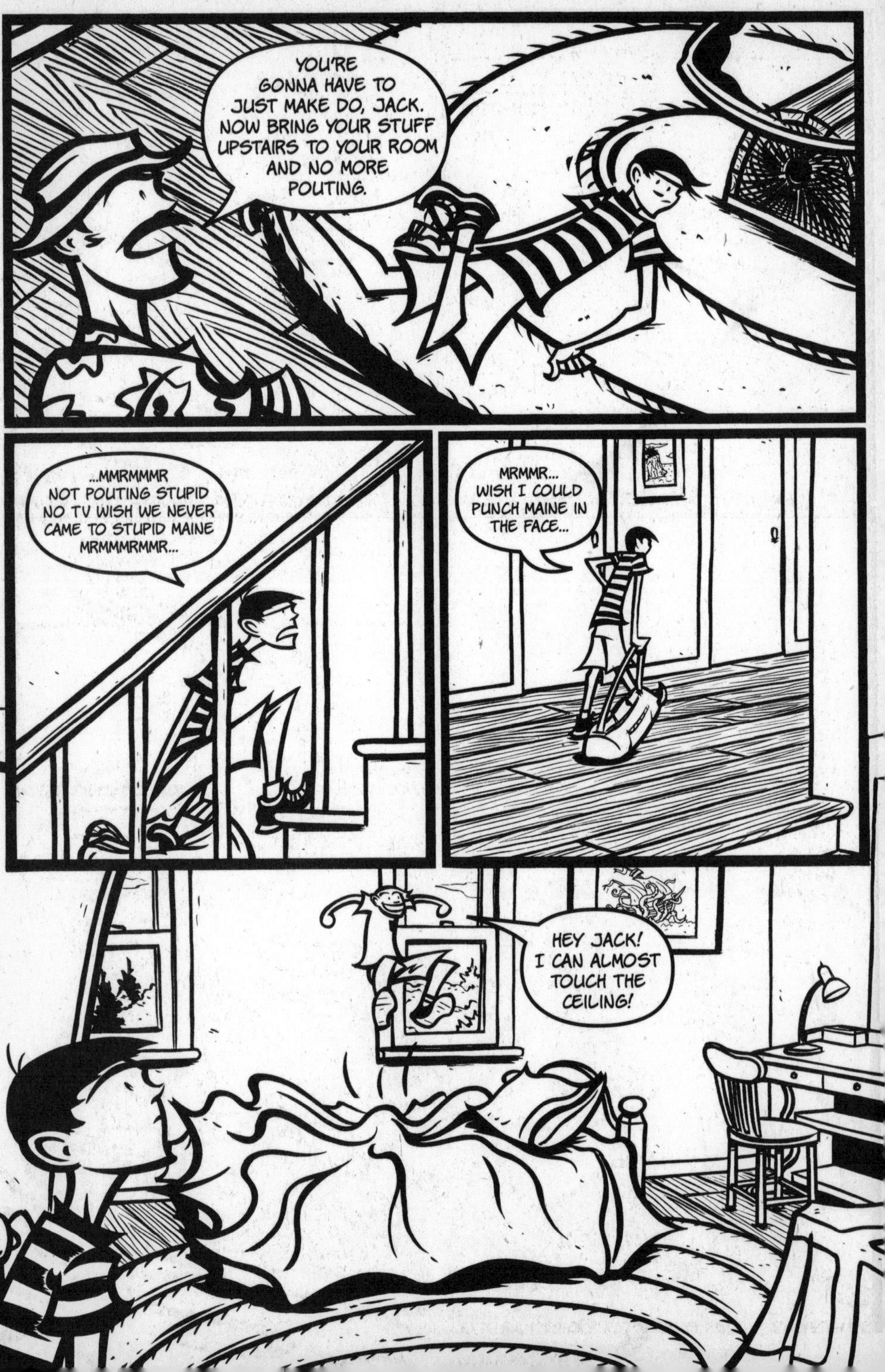
YOU'RE GONNA HAVE TO JUST MAKE DO, JACK. NOW BRING YOUR STUFF UPSTAIRS TO YOUR ROOM AND NO MORE POUTING.
...MMRMMMR NOT POUTING STUPID NO TV WISH WE NEVER CAME TO STUPID MAINE MRMMMRMMR...
MRMMR... WISH I COULD PUNCH MAINE IN THE FACE...
HEY JACK! I CAN ALMOST TOUCH THE CEILING!

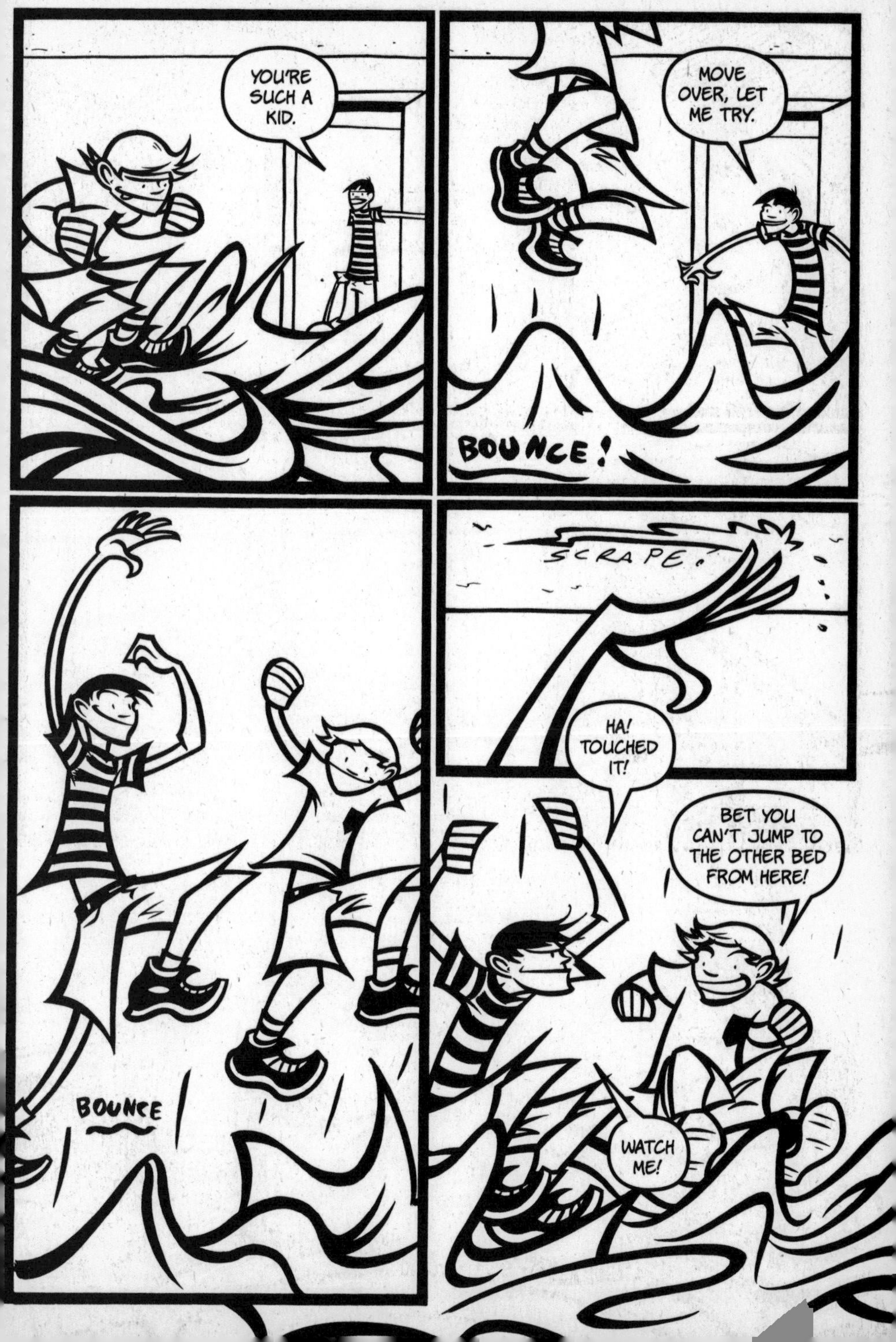

YOU'RE SUCH A KID.
MOVE OVER, LET ME TRY.
BOUNCE!
BOUNCE
SCRAPE.
HA! TOUCHED IT!
BET YOU CAN'T JUMP TO THE OTHER BED FROM HERE!
WATCH ME!

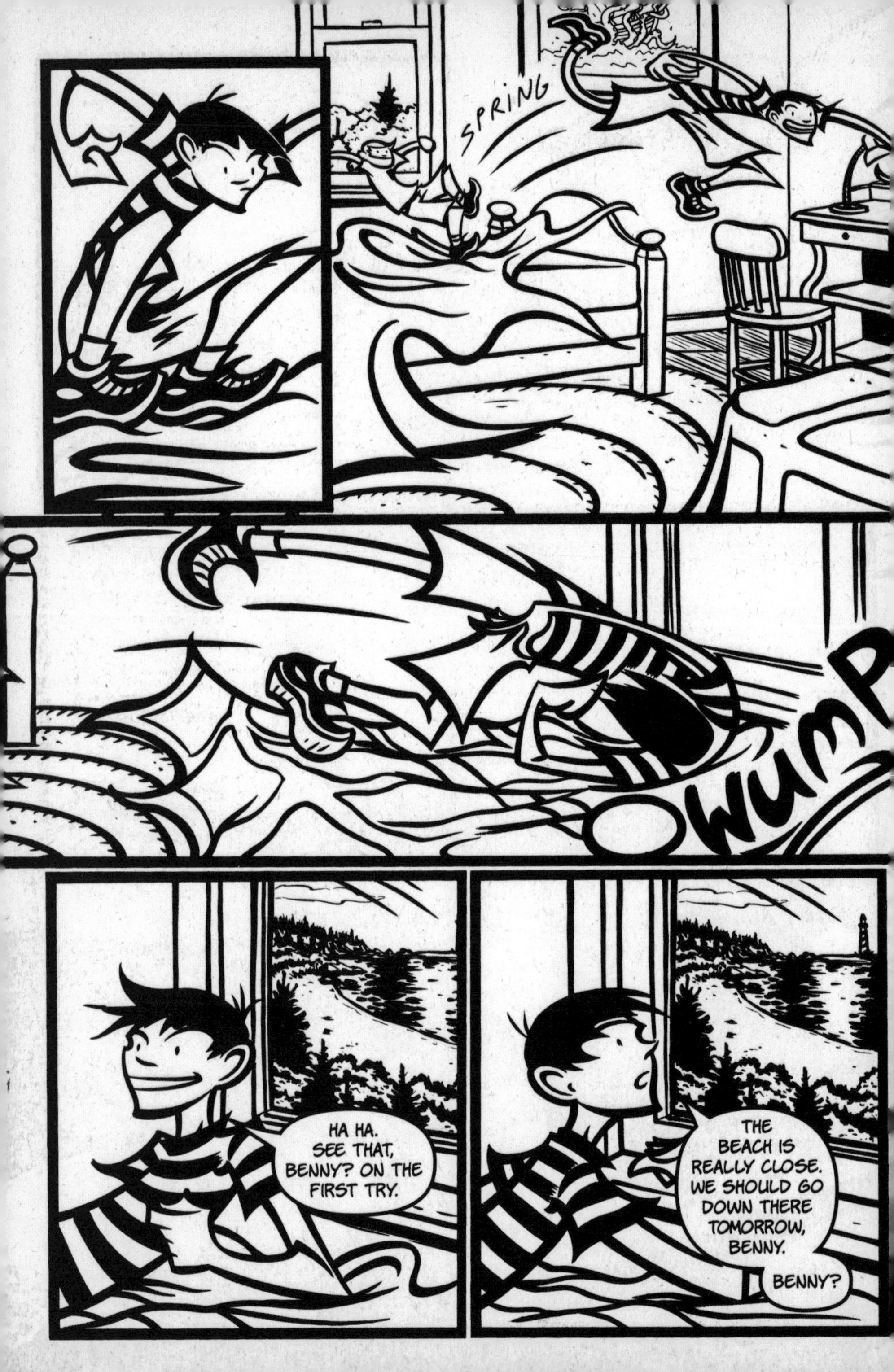
SPRING
WUMP
HA HA. SEE THAT, BENNY? ON THE FIRST TRY.
THE BEACH IS REALLY CLOSE. WE SHOULD GO DOWN THERE TOMORROW, BENNY.
BENNY?

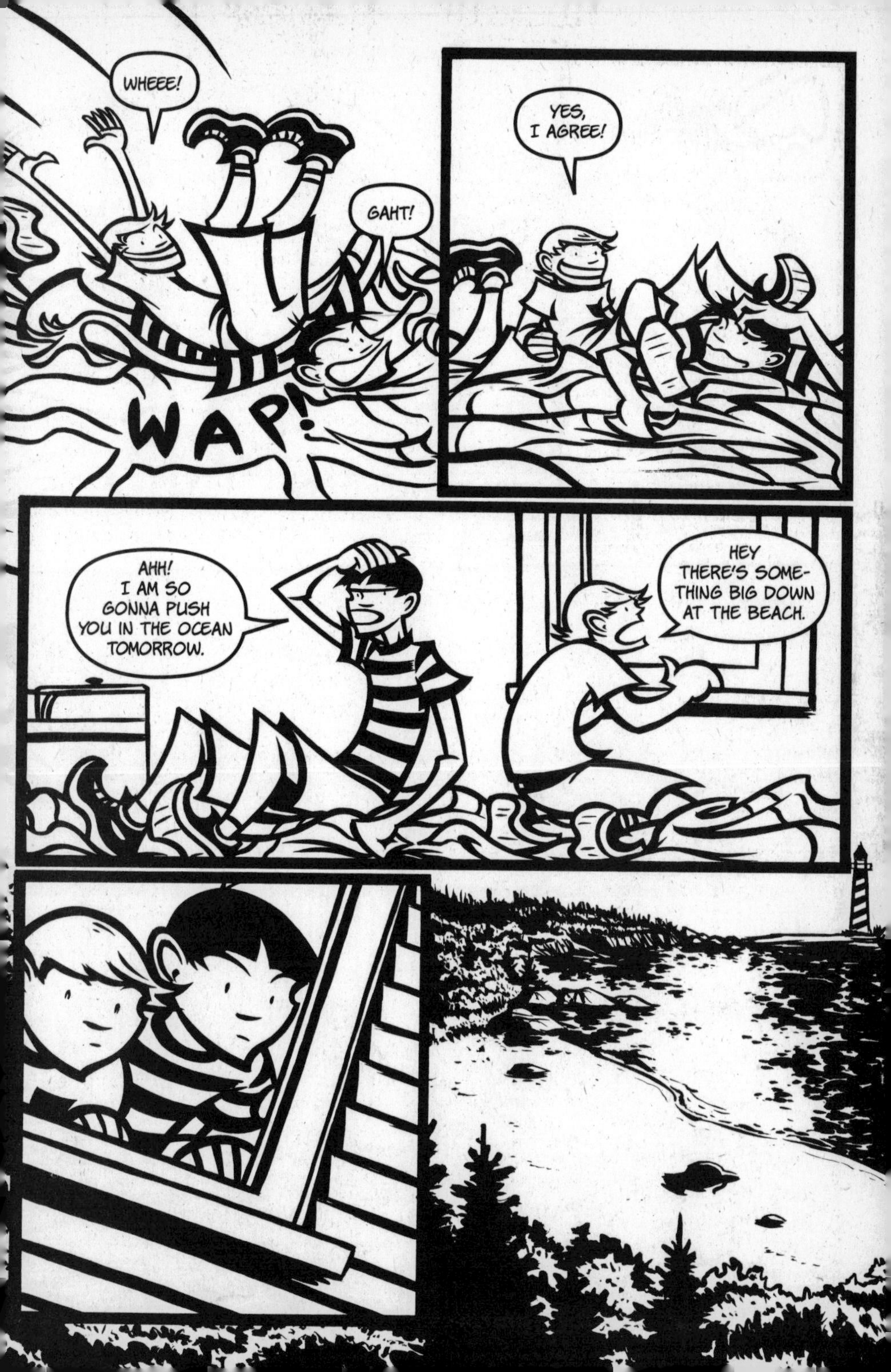
WHEEE!
GAHT!
WAP!
YES, I AGREE!
AHH! I AM SO GONNA PUSH YOU IN THE OCEAN TOMORROW.
HEY THERE'S SOME-THING BIG DOWN AT THE BEACH.

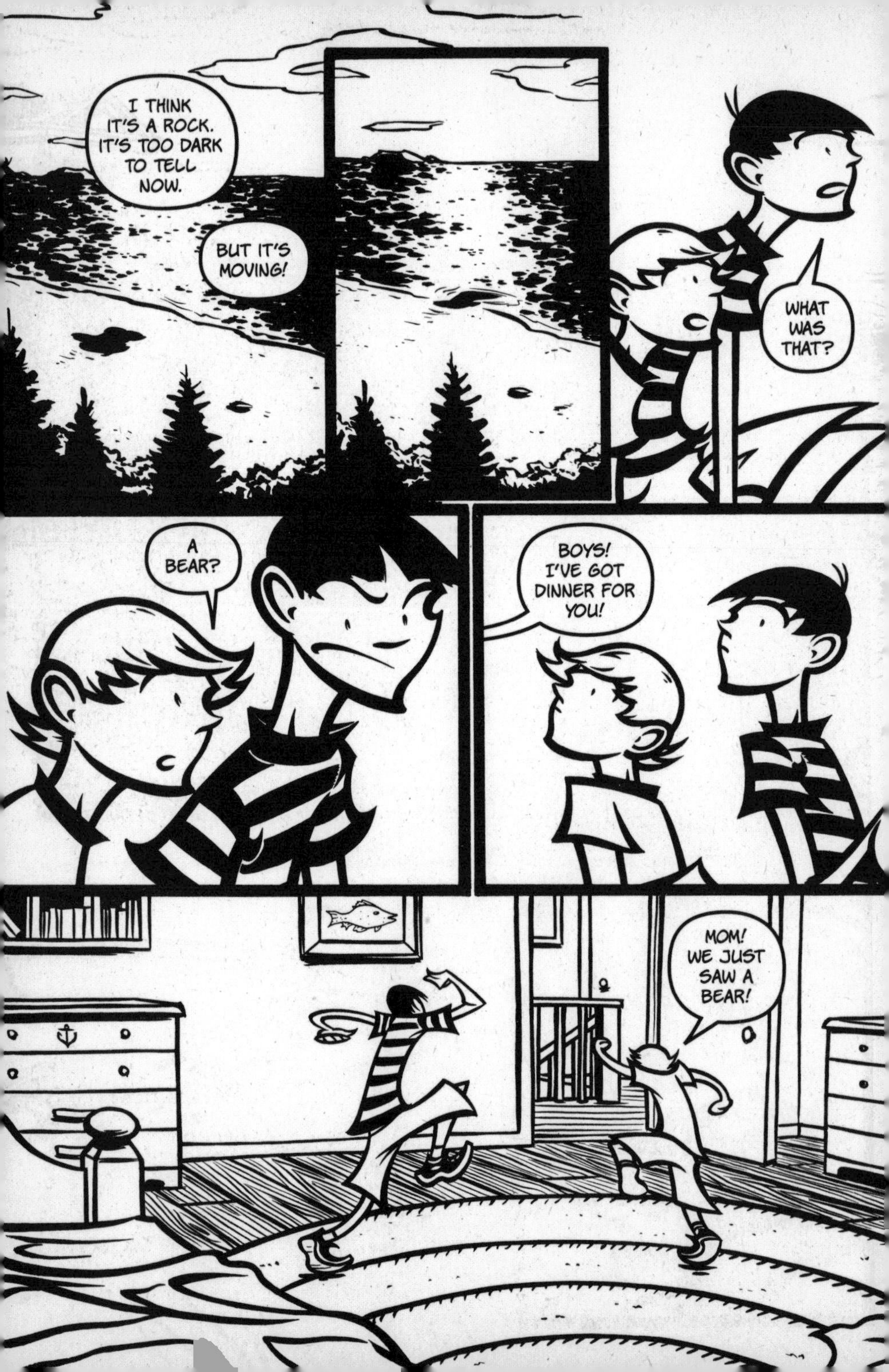
I THINK IT'S A ROCK. IT'S TOO DARK TO TELL NOW.
BUT IT'S MOVING!
WHAT WAS THAT?
A BEAR?
BOYS! I'VE GOT DINNER FOR YOU!
MOM! WE JUST SAW A BEAR!

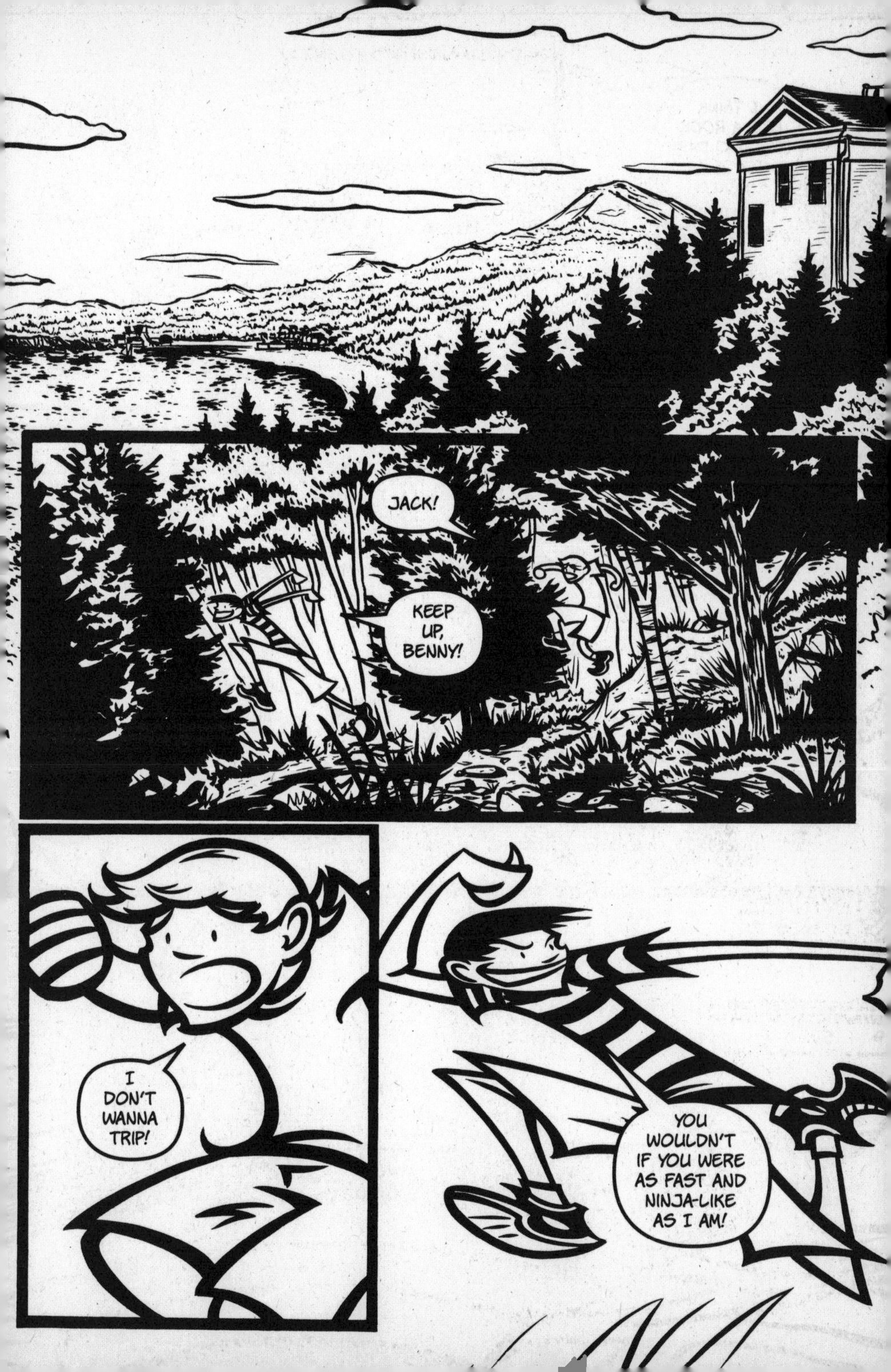
JACK!
KEEP UP, BENNY!
I DON'T WANNA TRIP!
YOU WOULDN'T IF YOU WERE AS FAST AND NINJA-LIKE AS I AM!

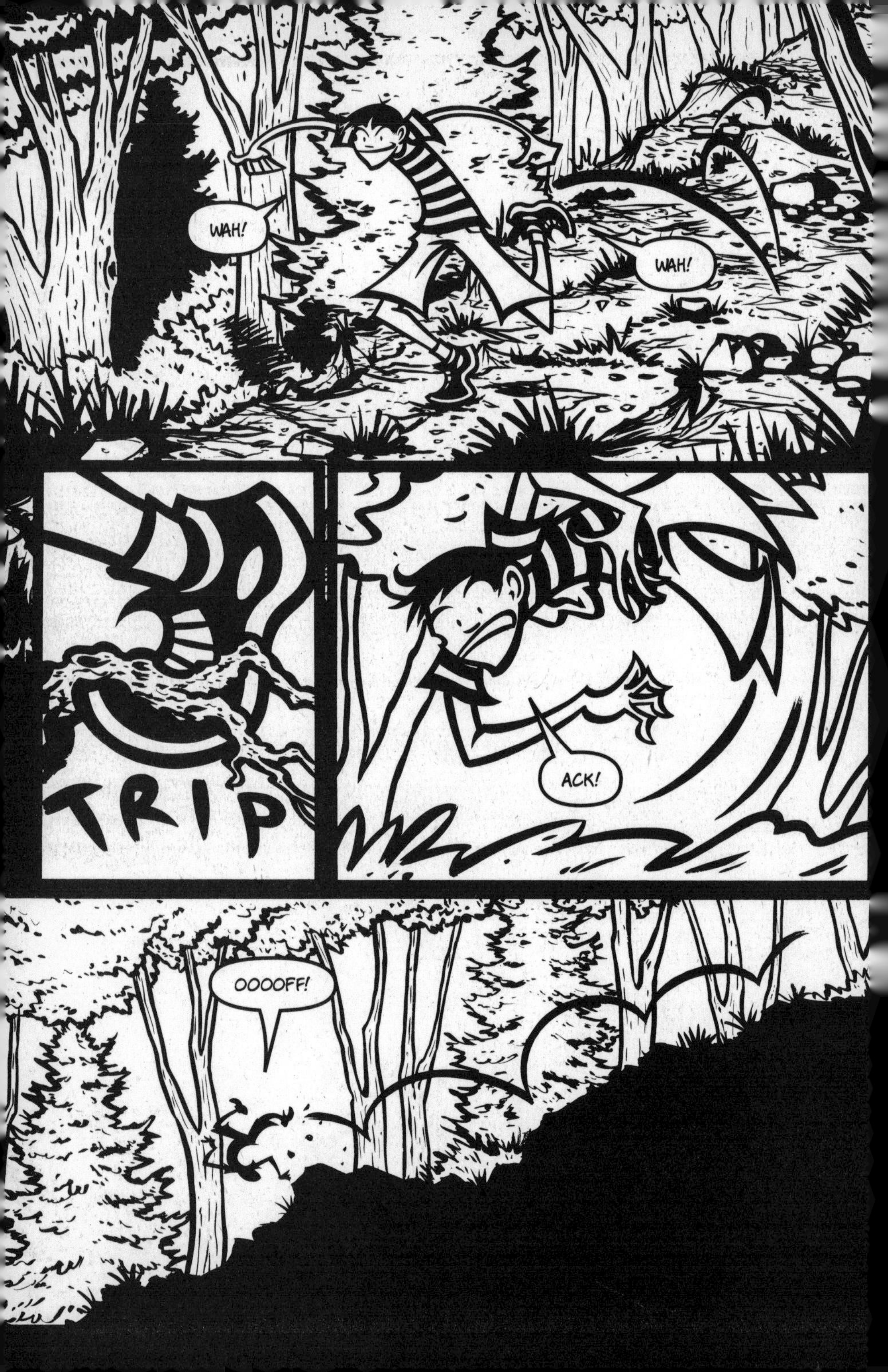
WAH!
WAH!
TRIP
ACK!
OOOOFF!

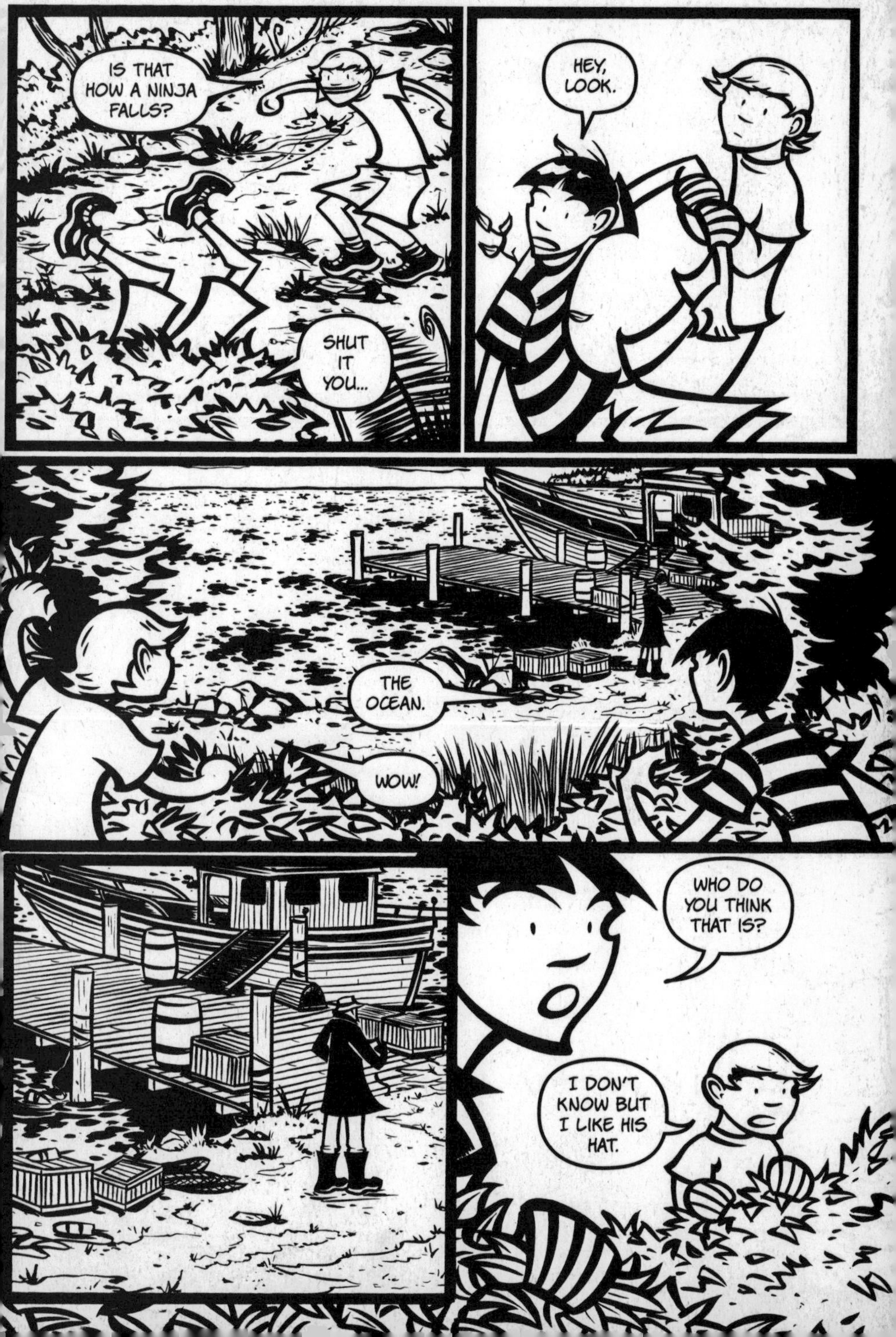
IS THAT HOW A NINJA FALLS?
SHUT IT YOU...
HEY, LOOK.
THE OCEAN.
WOW!
WHO DO YOU THINK THAT IS?
I DON'T KNOW BUT I LIKE HIS HAT.

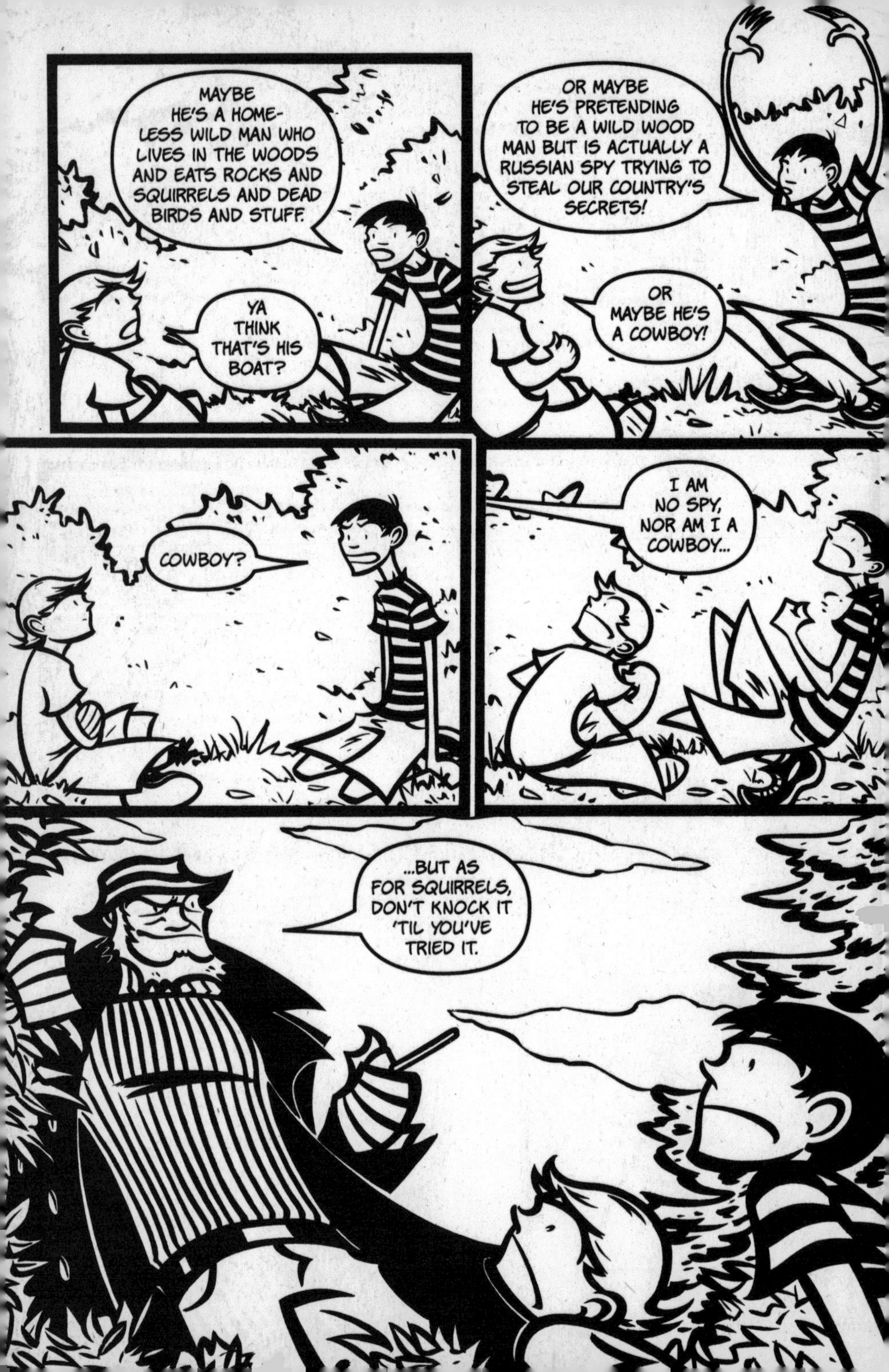
MAYBE HE'S A HOME-LESS WILD MAN WHO LIVES IN THE WOODS AND EATS ROCKS AND SQUIRRELS AND DEAD BIRDS AND STUFF.
YA THINK THAT'S HIS BOAT?
OR MAYBE HE'S PRETENDING TO BE A WILD WOOD MAN BUT IS ACTUALLY A RUSSIAN SPY TRYING TO STEAL OUR COUNTRY'S SECRETS!
OR MAYBE HE'S A COWBOY!
COWBOY?
I AM NO SPY, NOR AM I A COWBOY...
...BUT AS FOR SQUIRRELS, DON'T KNOCK IT 'TIL YOU'VE TRIED IT.

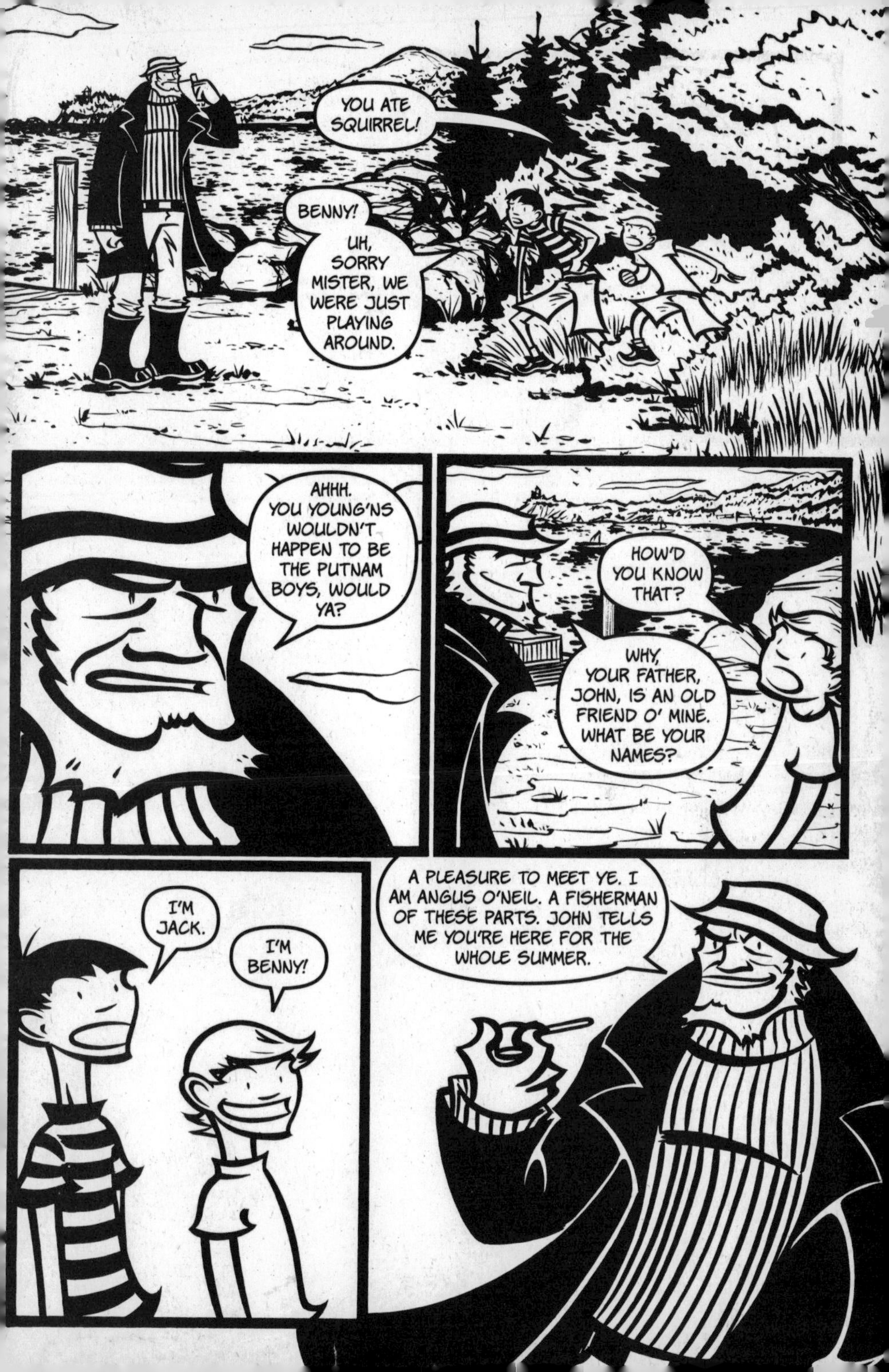
YOU ATE SQUIRREL!
BENNY!
UH, SORRY MISTER, WE WERE JUST PLAYING AROUND.
AHHH. YOU YOUNG'NS WOULDN'T HAPPEN TO BE THE PUTNAM BOYS, WOULD YA?
HOW'D YOU KNOW THAT?
WHY, YOUR FATHER, JOHN, IS AN OLD FRIEND O' MINE. WHAT BE YOUR NAMES?
I'M JACK.
I'M BENNY!
A PLEASURE TO MEET YE. I AM ANGUS O'NEIL. A FISHERMAN OF THESE PARTS. JOHN TELLS ME YOU'RE HERE FOR THE WHOLE SUMMER.

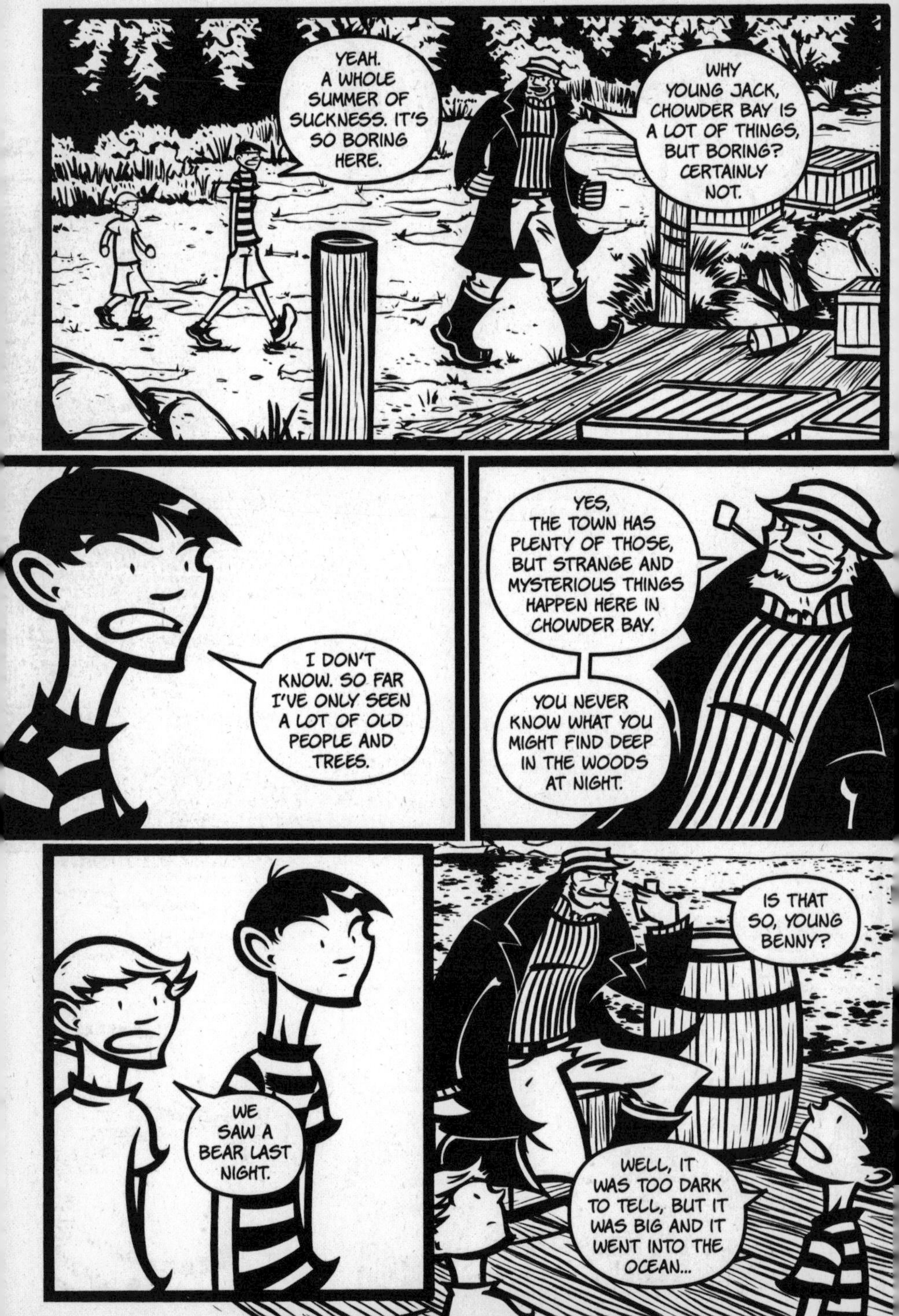
YEAH. A WHOLE SUMMER OF SUCKNESS. IT'S SO BORING HERE.
WHY YOUNG JACK, CHOWDER BAY IS A LOT OF THINGS, BUT BORING? CERTAINLY NOT.
I DON'T KNOW. SO FAR I'VE ONLY SEEN A LOT OF OLD PEOPLE AND TREES.
YES, THE TOWN HAS PLENTY OF THOSE, BUT STRANGE AND MYSTERIOUS THINGS HAPPEN HERE IN CHOWDER BAY.
YOU NEVER KNOW WHAT YOU MIGHT FIND DEEP IN THE WOODS AT NIGHT.
WE SAW A BEAR LAST NIGHT.
IS THAT SO, YOUNG BENNY?
WELL, IT WAS TOO DARK TO TELL, BUT IT WAS BIG AND IT WENT INTO THE OCEAN...

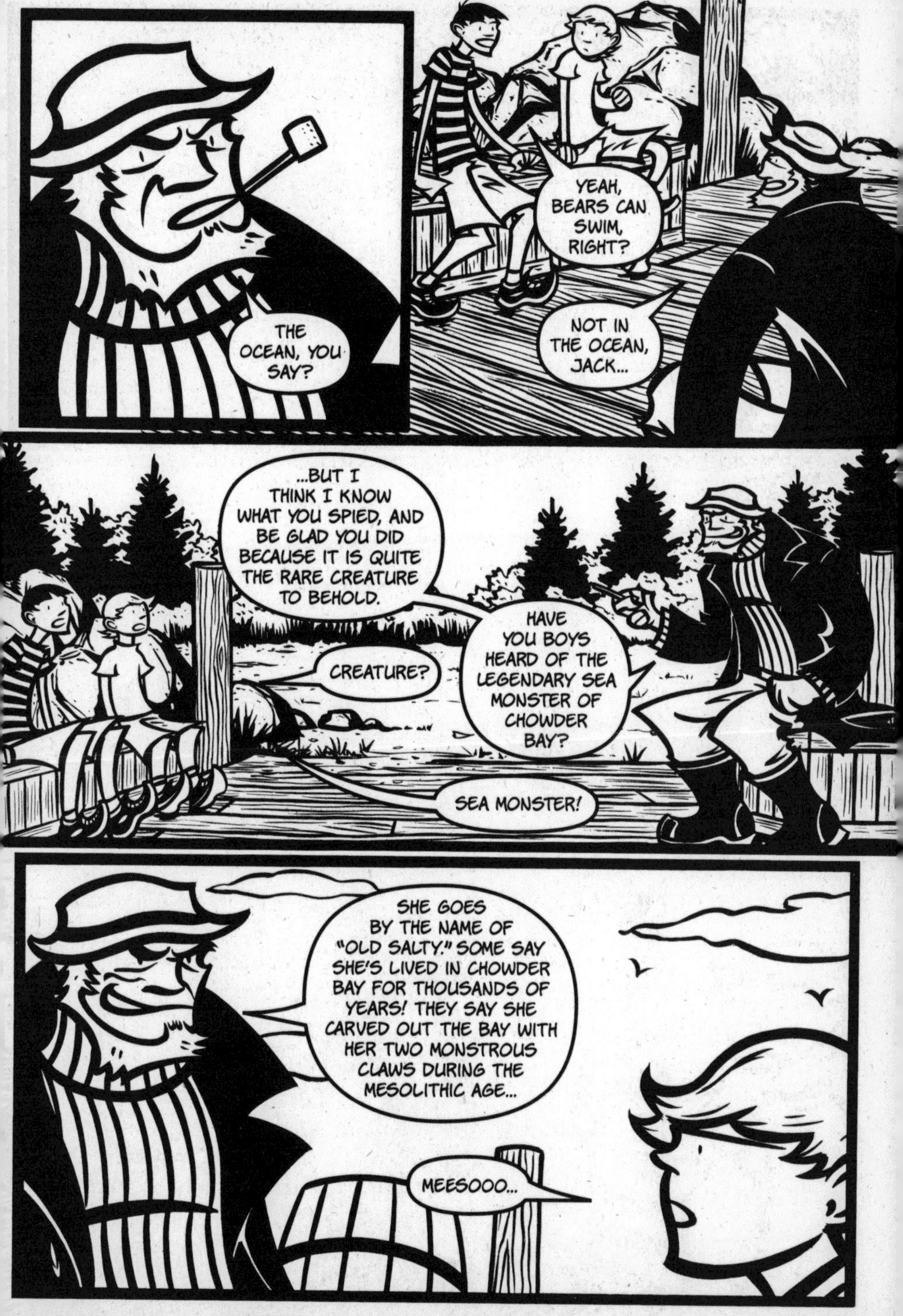
THE OCEAN, YOU SAY?
YEAH, BEARS CAN SWIM, RIGHT?
NOT IN THE OCEAN, JACK...
...BUT I THINK I KNOW WHAT YOU SPIED, AND BE GLAD YOU DID BECAUSE IT IS QUITE THE RARE CREATURE TO BEHOLD.
CREATURE?
HAVE YOU BOYS HEARD OF THE LEGENDARY SEA MONSTER OF CHOWDER BAY?
SEA MONSTER!
SHE GOES BY THE NAME OF "OLD SALTY." SOME SAY SHE'S LIVED IN CHOWDER BAY FOR THOUSANDS OF YEARS! THEY SAY SHE CARVED OUT THE BAY WITH HER TWO MONSTROUS CLAWS DURING THE MESOLITHIC AGE...
MEESOOO...

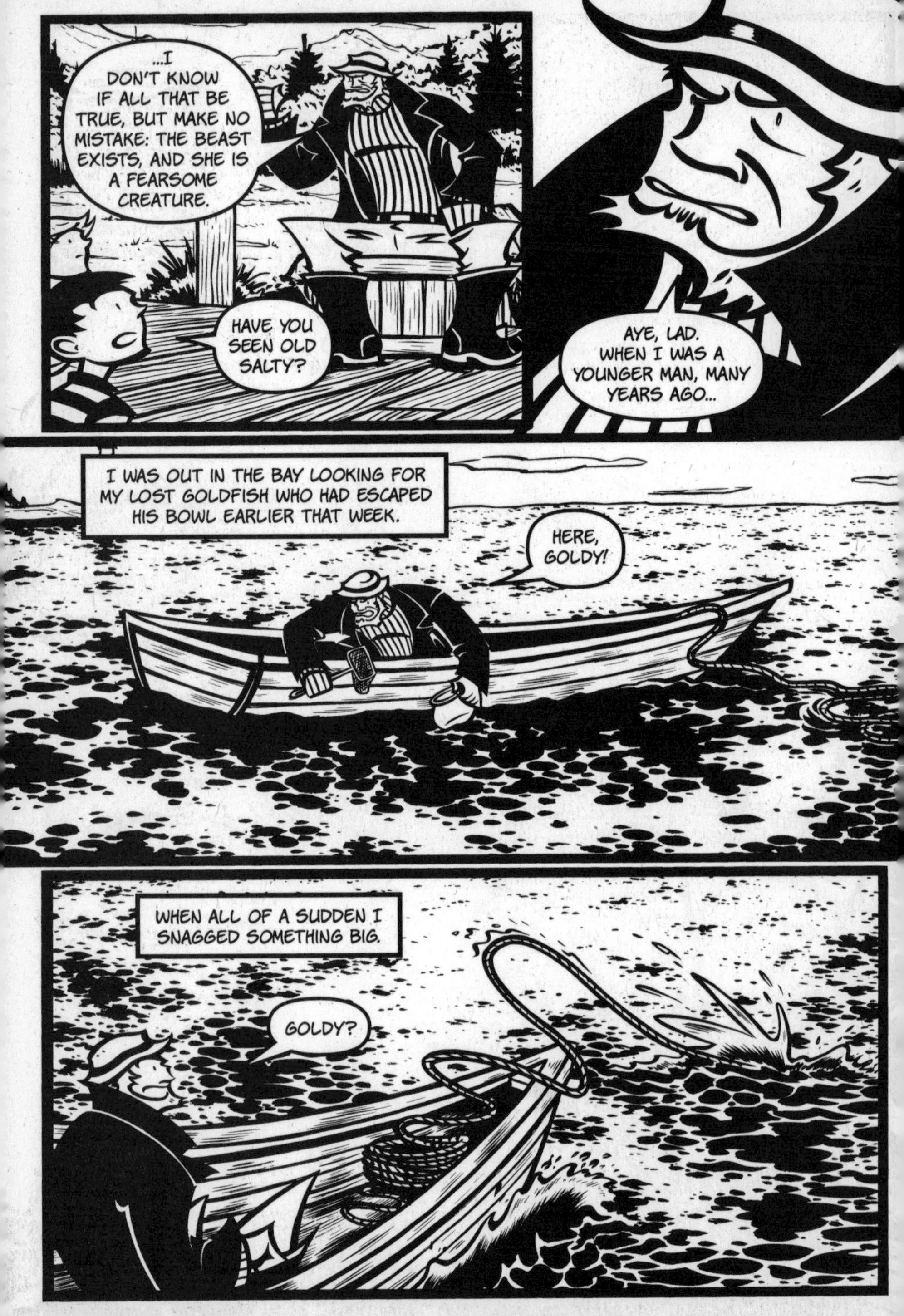
...I DON'T KNOW IF ALL THAT BE TRUE, BUT MAKE NO MISTAKE: THE BEAST EXISTS, AND SHE IS A FEARSOME CREATURE.
HAVE YOU SEEN OLD SALTY?
AYE, LAD. WHEN I WAS A YOUNGER MAN, MANY YEARS AGO...
I WAS OUT IN THE BAY LOOKING FOR MY LOST GOLDFISH WHO HAD ESCAPED HIS BOWL EARLIER THAT WEEK.
HERE, GOLDY!
WHEN ALL OF A SUDDEN I SNAGGED SOMETHING BIG.
GOLDY?

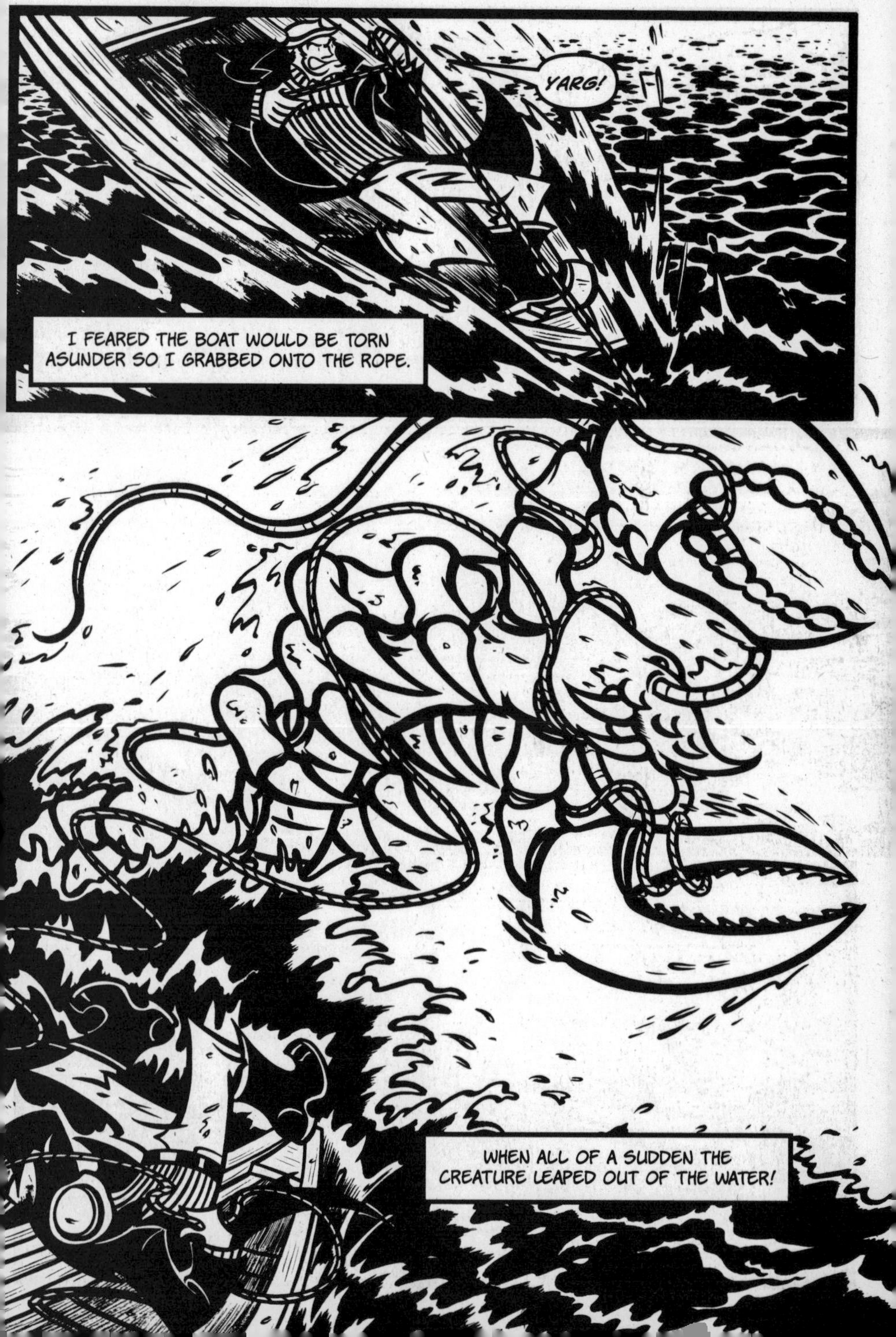
YARG!
I FEARED THE BOAT WOULD BE TORN ASUNDER SO I GRABBED ONTO THE ROPE.
WHEN ALL OF A SUDDEN THE CREATURE LEAPED OUT OF THE WATER!

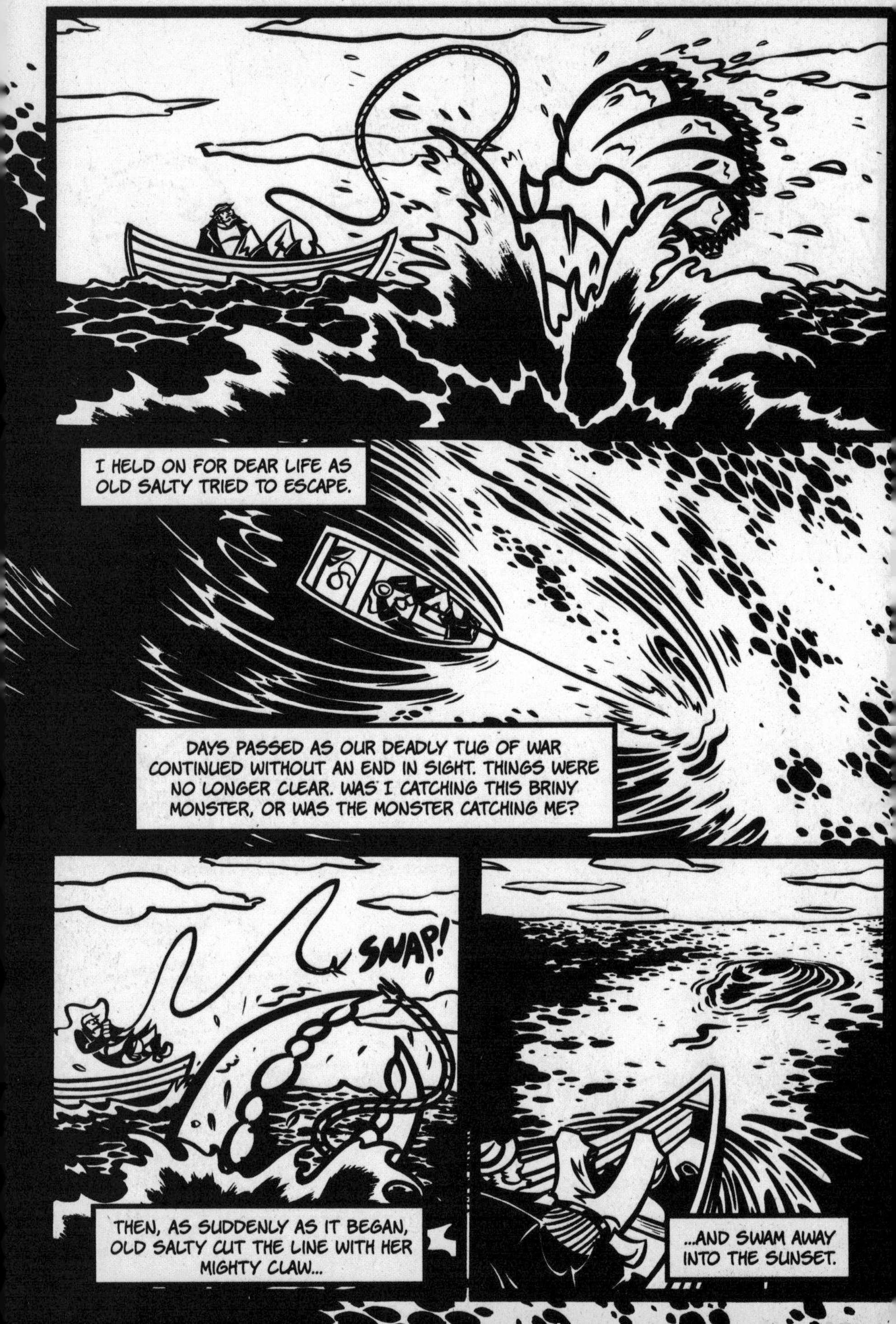
I HELD ON FOR DEAR LIFE AS OLD SALTY TRIED TO ESCAPE.
DAYS PASSED AS OUR DEADLY TUG OF WAR CONTINUED WITHOUT AN END IN SIGHT. THINGS WERE NO LONGER CLEAR. WAS I CATCHING THIS BRINY MONSTER, OR WAS THE MONSTER CATCHING ME?
SNAP!
THEN, AS SUDDENLY AS IT BEGAN, OLD SALTY CUT THE LINE WITH HER MIGHTY CLAW...
...AND SWAM AWAY INTO THE SUNSET.

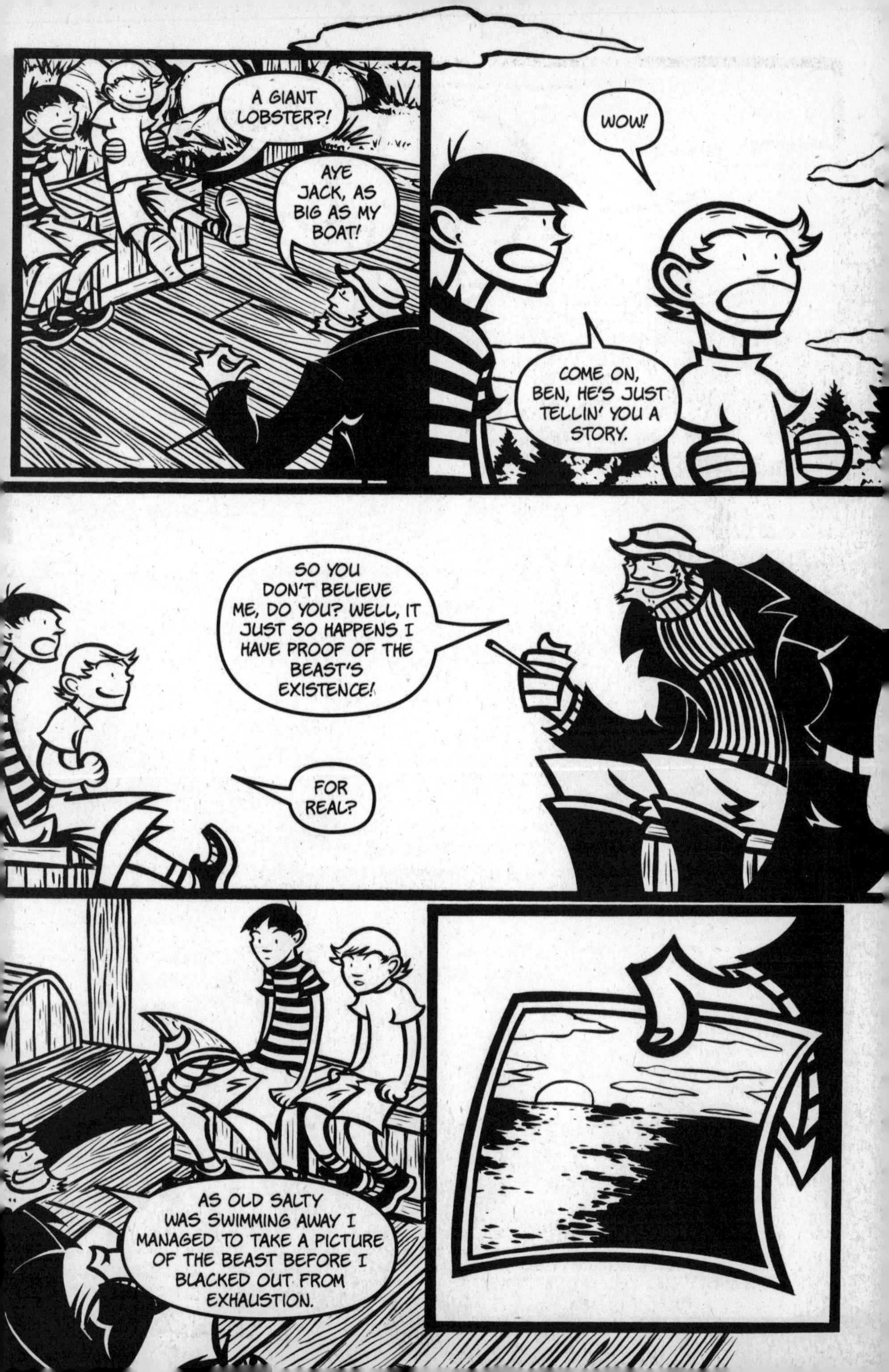
A GIANT LOBSTER?!
AYE JACK, AS BIG AS MY BOAT!
WOW!
COME ON, BEN, HE'S JUST TELLIN' YOU A STORY.
SO YOU DON'T BELIEVE ME, DO YOU? WELL, IT JUST SO HAPPENS I HAVE PROOF OF THE BEAST'S EXISTENCE!
FOR REAL?
AS OLD SALTY WAS SWIMMING AWAY I MANAGED TO TAKE A PICTURE OF THE BEAST BEFORE I BLACKED OUT FROM EXHAUSTION.

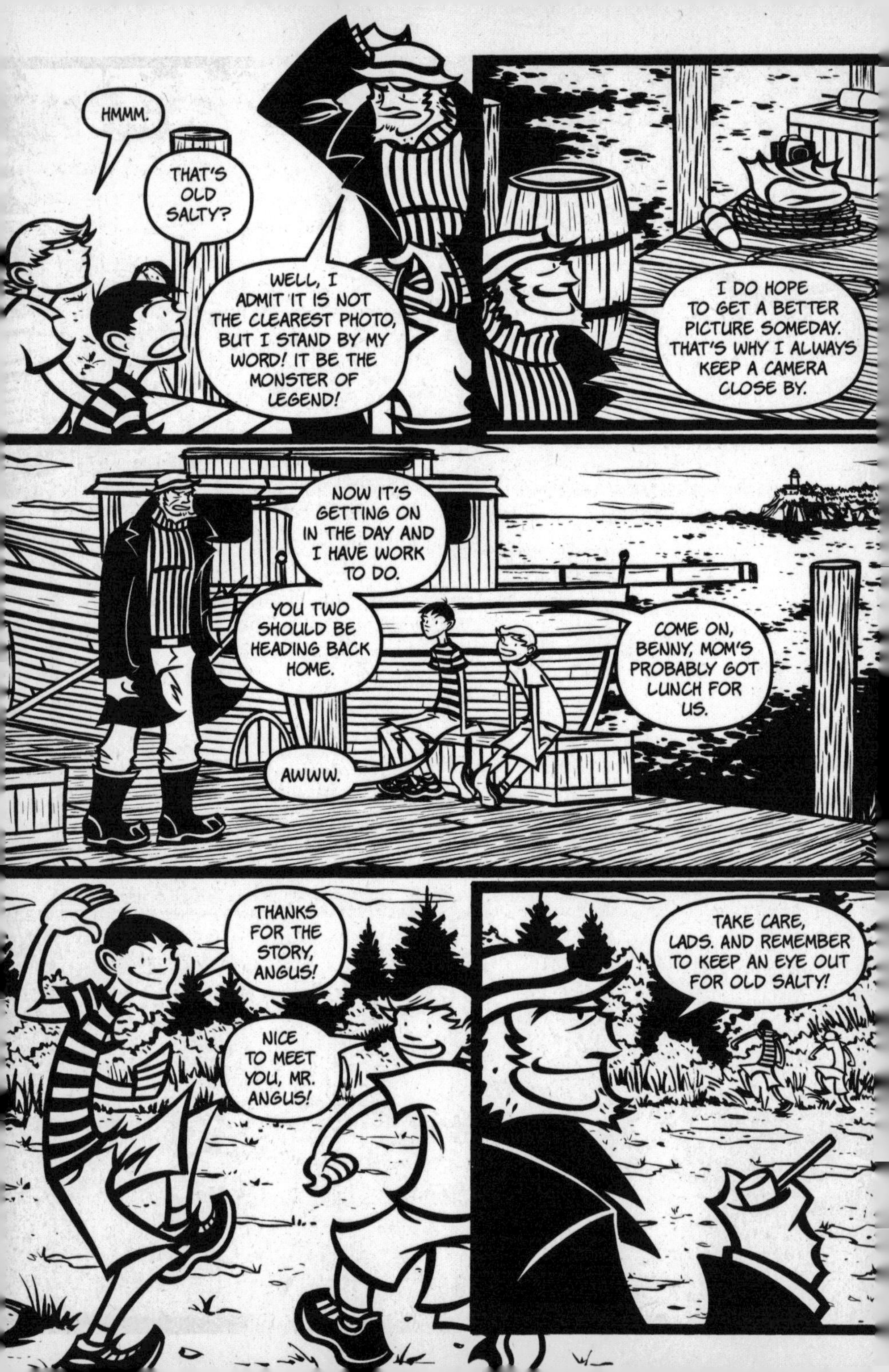
HMMM.
THAT'S OLD SALTY?
WELL, I ADMIT IT IS NOT THE CLEAREST PHOTO, BUT I STAND BY MY WORD! IT BE THE MONSTER OF LEGEND!
I DO HOPE TO GET A BETTER PICTURE SOMEDAY. THAT'S WHY I ALWAYS KEEP A CAMERA CLOSE BY.
NOW IT'S GETTING ON IN THE DAY AND I HAVE WORK TO DO.
YOU TWO SHOULD BE HEADING BACK HOME.
COME ON, BENNY, MOM'S PROBABLY GOT LUNCH FOR US.
AWWW.
THANKS FOR THE STORY, ANGUS!
NICE TO MEET YOU, MR. ANGUS!
TAKE CARE, LADS. AND REMEMBER TO KEEP AN EYE OUT FOR OLD SALTY!

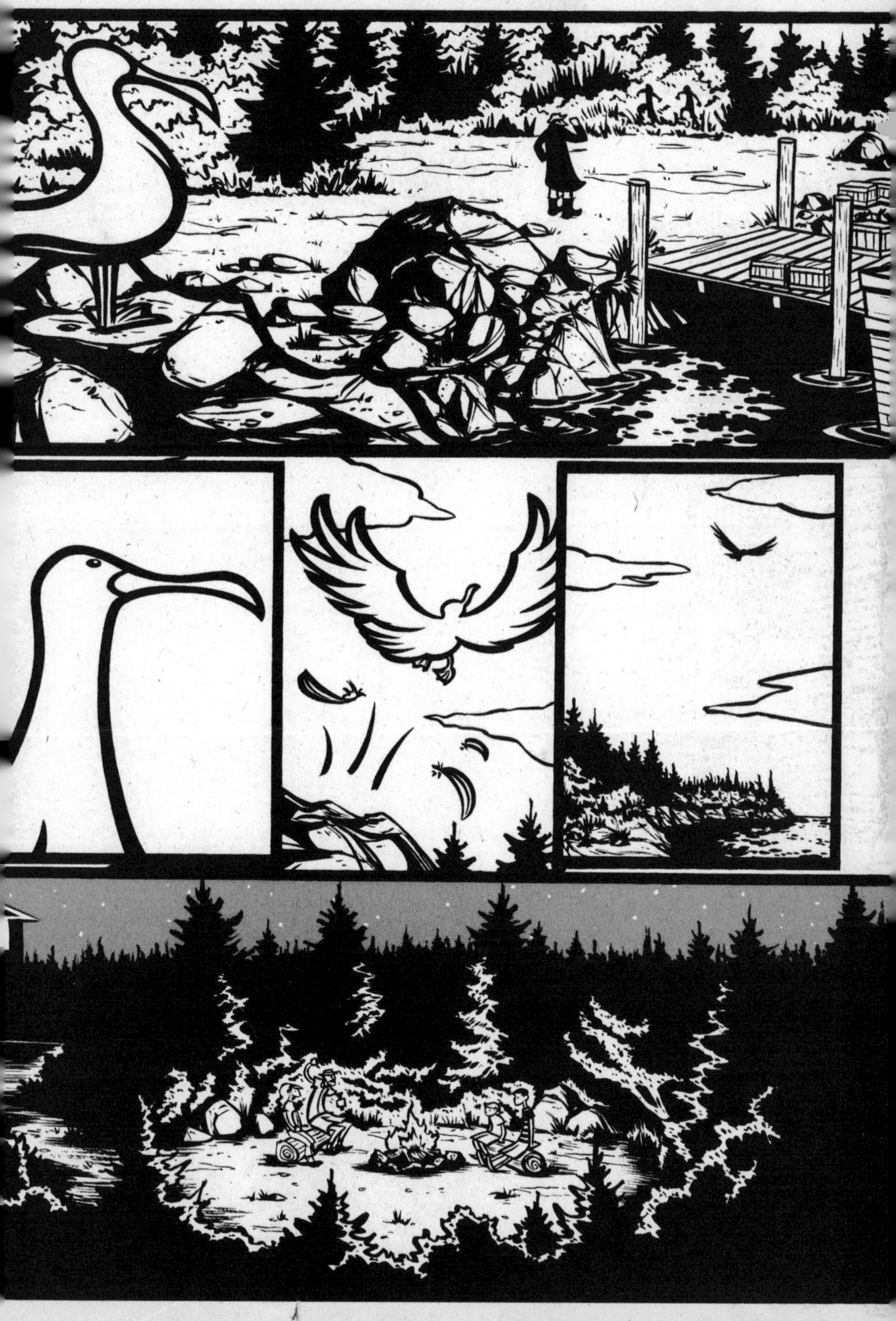

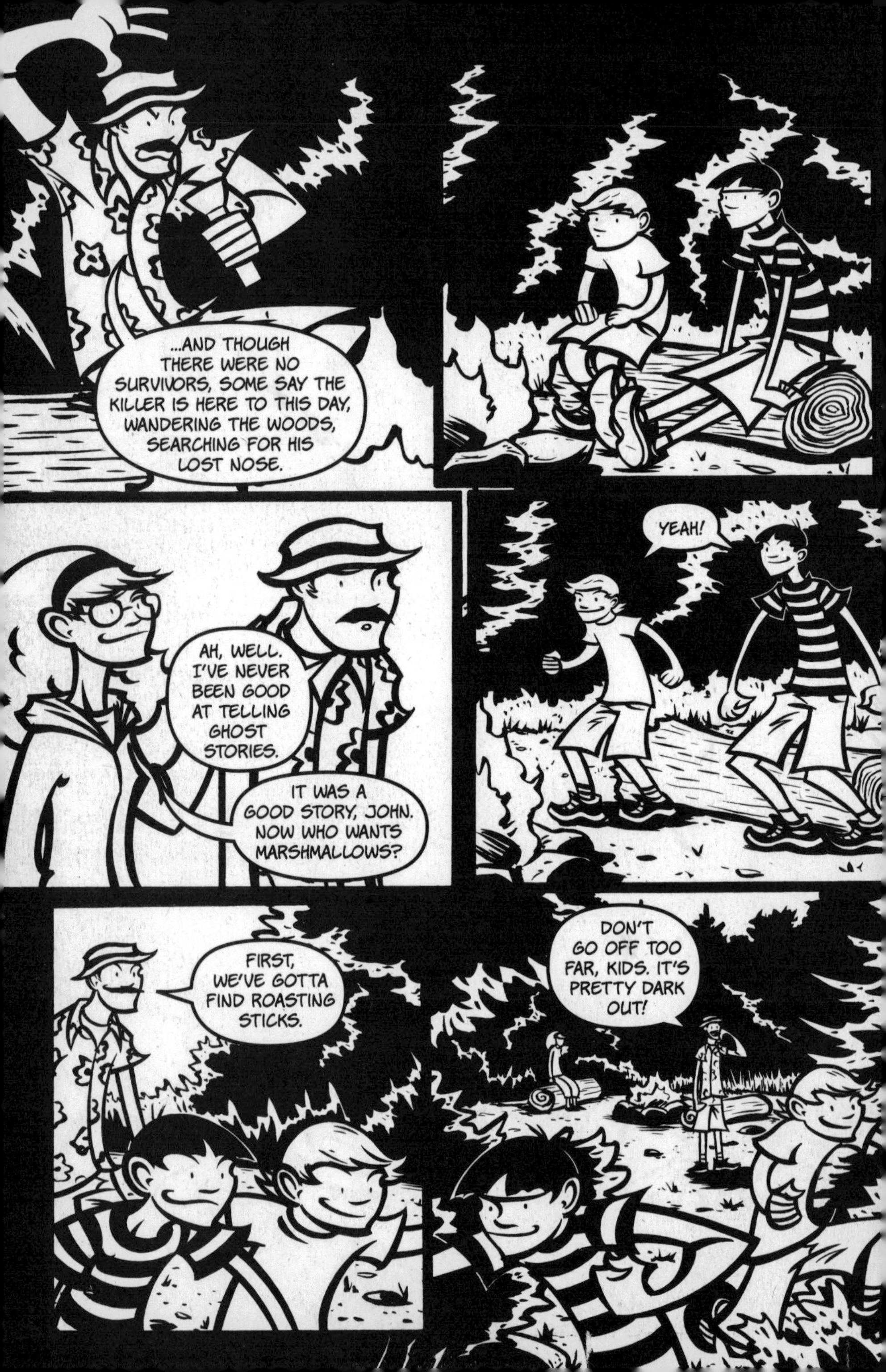
...AND THOUGH THERE WERE NO SURVIVORS, SOME SAY THE KILLER IS HERE TO THIS DAY, WANDERING THE WOODS, SEARCHING FOR HIS LOST NOSE.
AH, WELL. I'VE NEVER BEEN GOOD AT TELLING GHOST STORIES.
IT WAS A GOOD STORY, JOHN. NOW WHO WANTS MARSHMALLOWS?
YEAH!
FIRST, WE'VE GOTTA FIND ROASTING STICKS.
DON'T GO OFF TOO FAR, KIDS. IT'S PRETTY DARK OUT!

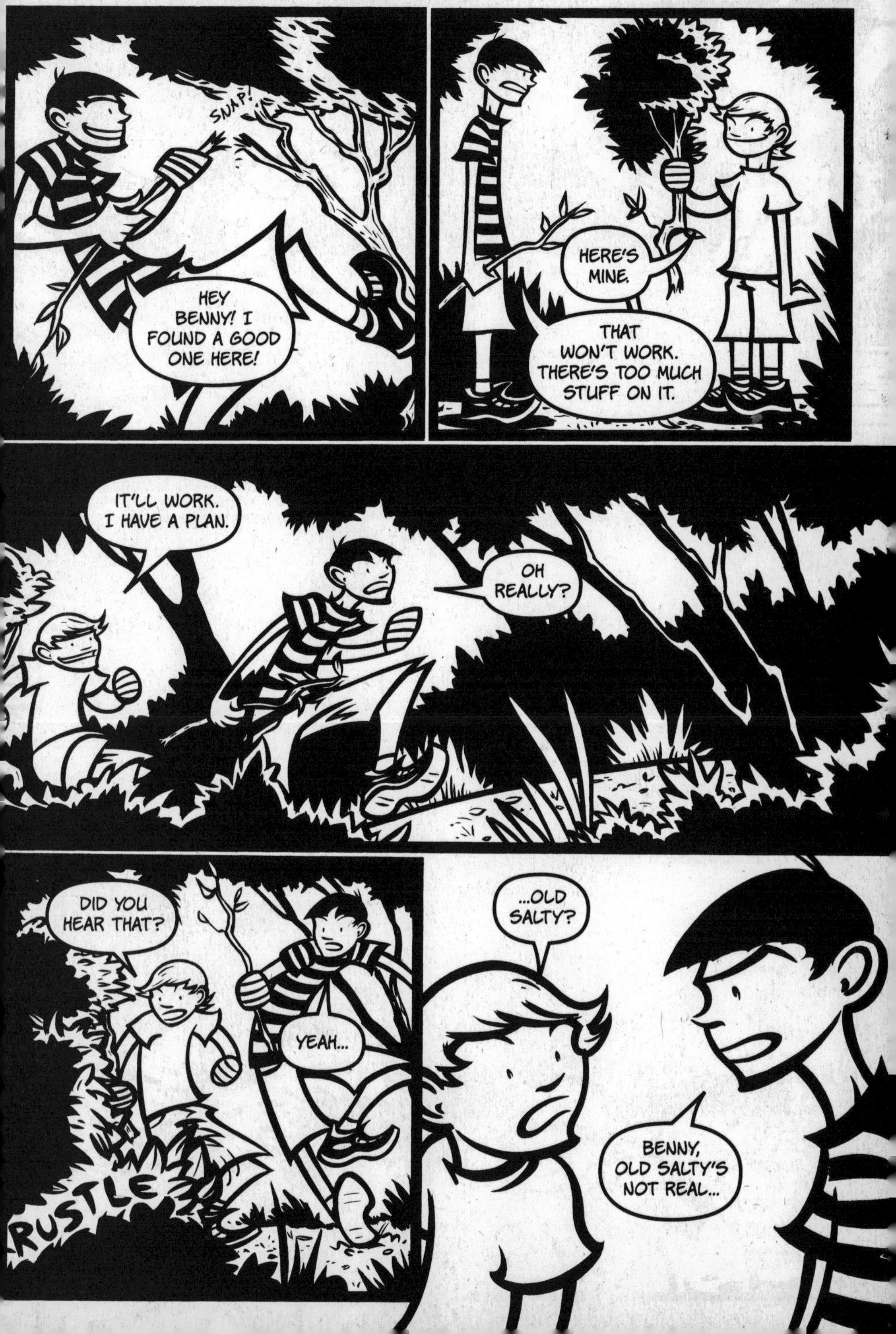
SNAP!
HEY BENNY! I FOUND A GOOD ONE HERE!
HERE'S MINE.
THAT WON'T WORK. THERE'S TOO MUCH STUFF ON IT.
IT'LL WORK. I HAVE A PLAN.
OH REALLY?
DID YOU HEAR THAT?
YEAH...
RUSTLE
...OLD SALTY?
BENNY, OLD SALTY'S NOT REAL...

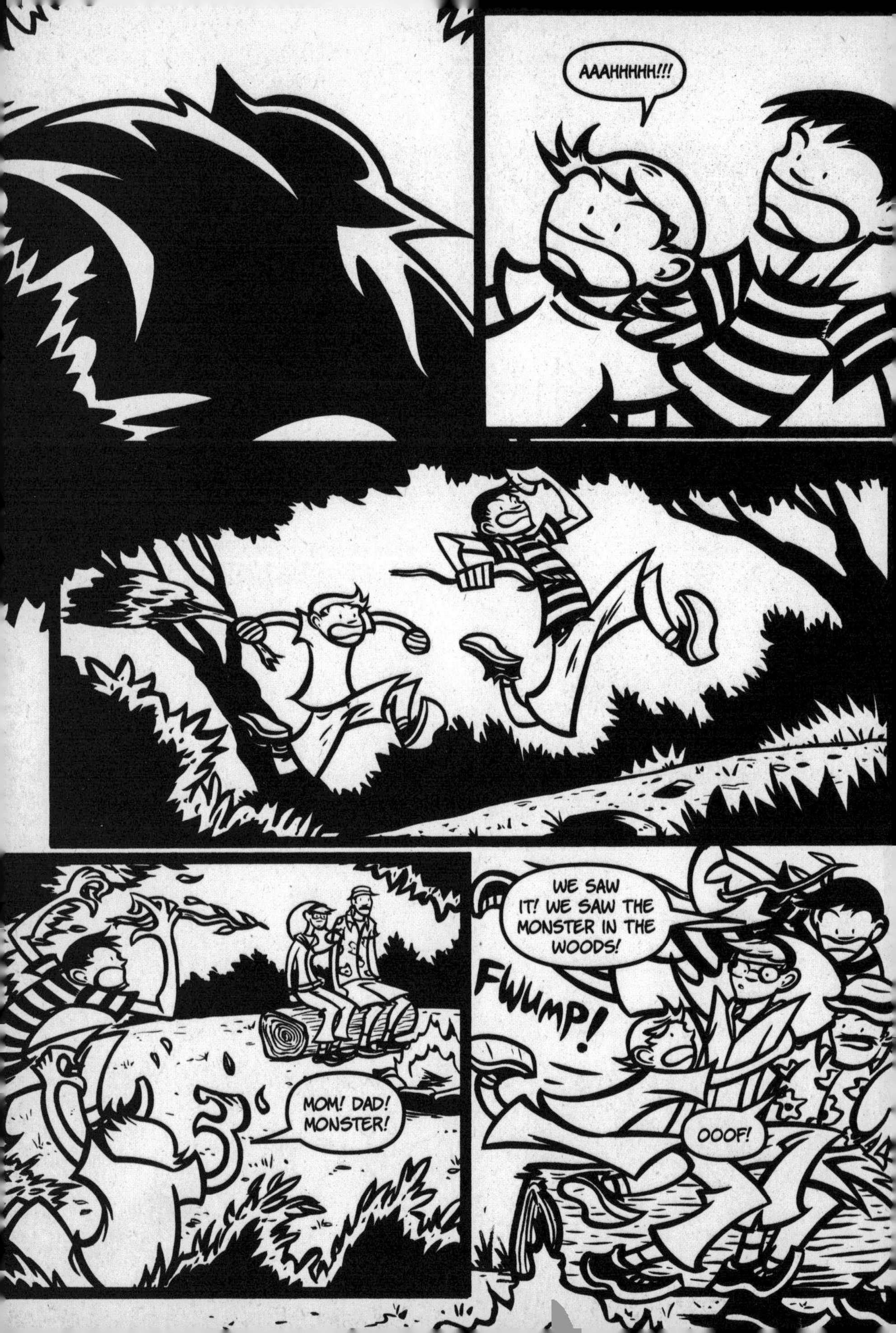
AAAHHHHH!!!
MOM! DAD! MONSTER!
WE SAW IT! WE SAW THE MONSTER IN THE WOODS!
FWUMP!
OOOF!

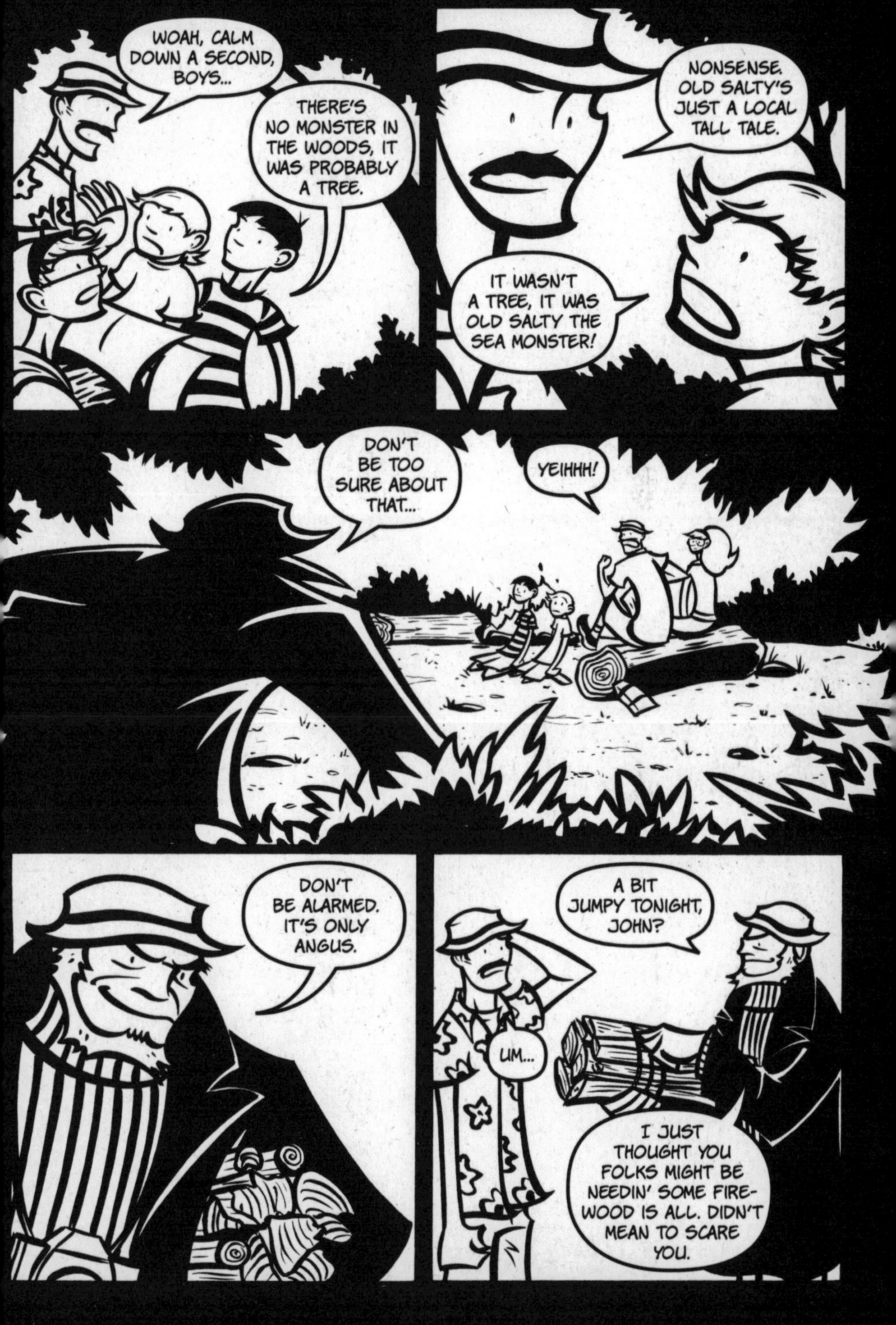
WOAH, CALM DOWN A SECOND, BOYS...
THERE'S NO MONSTER IN THE WOODS, IT WAS PROBABLY A TREE.
IT WASN'T A TREE, IT WAS OLD SALTY THE SEA MONSTER!
NONSENSE. OLD SALTY'S JUST A LOCAL TALL TALE.
DON'T BE TOO SURE ABOUT THAT...
YEIHHH!
DON'T BE ALARMED. IT'S ONLY ANGUS.
A BIT JUMPY TONIGHT, JOHN?
UM...
I JUST THOUGHT YOU FOLKS MIGHT BE NEEDIN' SOME FIRE-WOOD IS ALL. DIDN'T MEAN TO SCARE YOU.

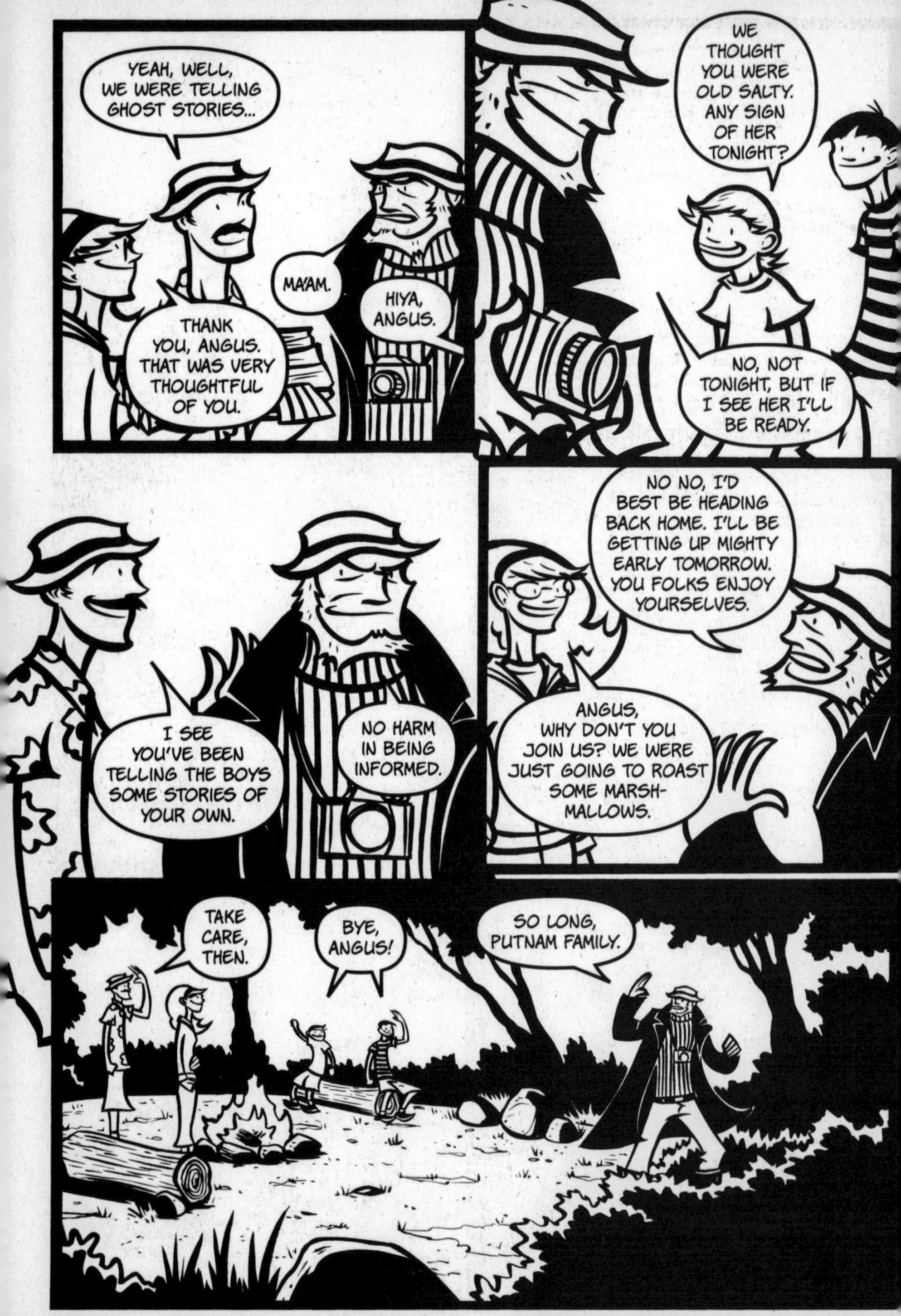
YEAH, WELL, WE WERE TELLING GHOST STORIES...
THANK YOU, ANGUS. THAT WAS VERY THOUGHTFUL OF YOU.
MA'AM.
HIYA, ANGUS.
WE THOUGHT YOU WERE OLD SALTY. ANY SIGN OF HER TONIGHT?
NO, NOT TONIGHT, BUT IF I SEE HER I'LL BE READY.
I SEE YOU'VE BEEN TELLING THE BOYS SOME STORIES OF YOUR OWN.
NO HARM IN BEING INFORMED.
ANGUS, WHY DON'T YOU JOIN US? WE WERE JUST GOING TO ROAST SOME MARSH-MALLOWS.
NO NO, I'D BEST BE HEADING BACK HOME. I'LL BE GETTING UP MIGHTY EARLY TOMORROW. YOU FOLKS ENJOY YOURSELVES.
TAKE CARE, THEN.
BYE, ANGUS!
SO LONG, PUTNAM FAMILY.

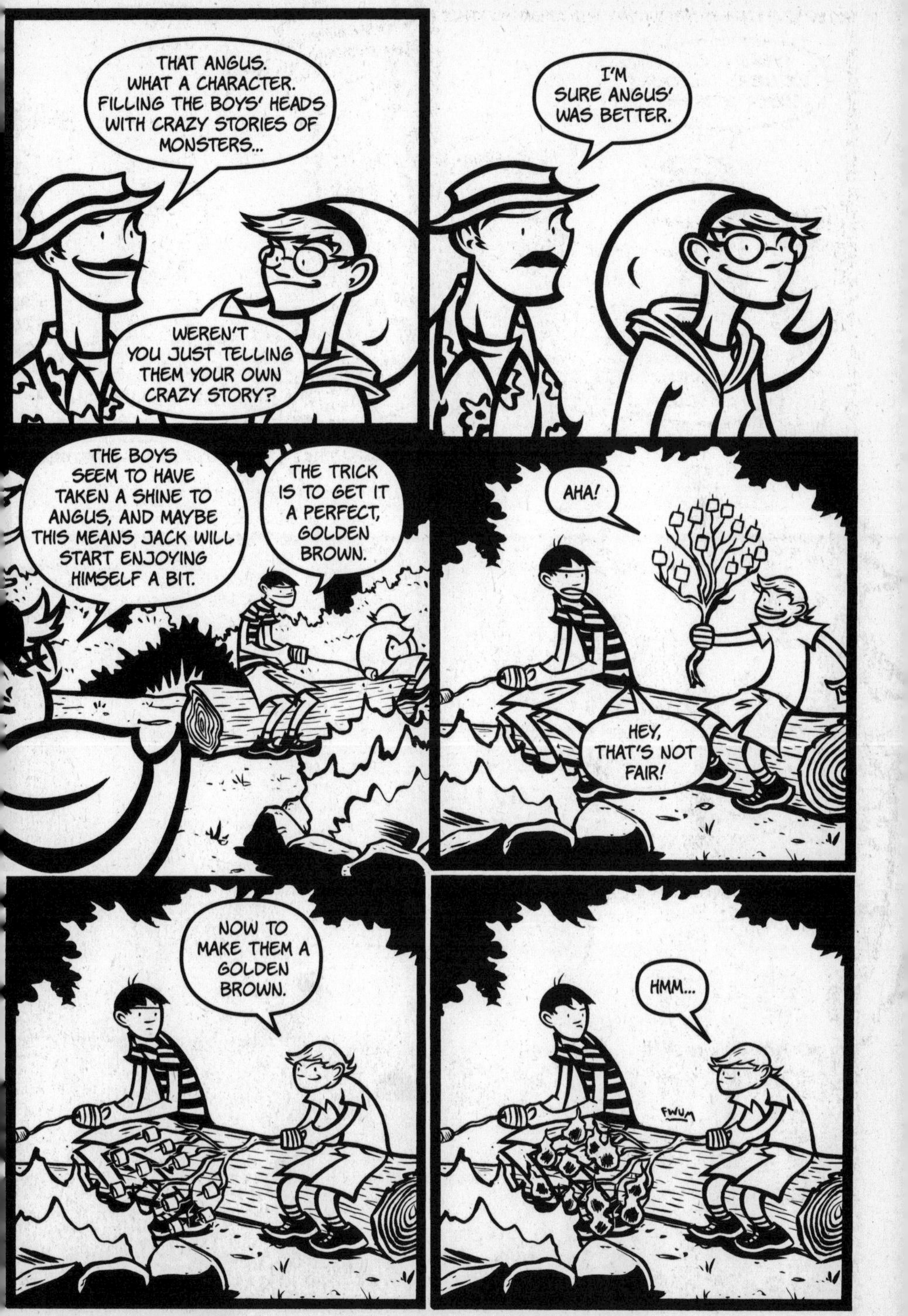
THAT ANGUS. WHAT A CHARACTER. FILLING THE BOYS' HEADS WITH CRAZY STORIES OF MONSTERS...
WEREN'T YOU JUST TELLING THEM YOUR OWN CRAZY STORY?
I'M SURE ANGUS' WAS BETTER.
THE BOYS SEEM TO HAVE TAKEN A SHINE TO ANGUS, AND MAYBE THIS MEANS JACK WILL START ENJOYING HIMSELF A BIT.
THE TRICK IS TO GET IT A PERFECT, GOLDEN BROWN.
AHA!
HEY, THAT'S NOT FAIR!
NOW TO MAKE THEM A GOLDEN BROWN.
HMM...
FWUM

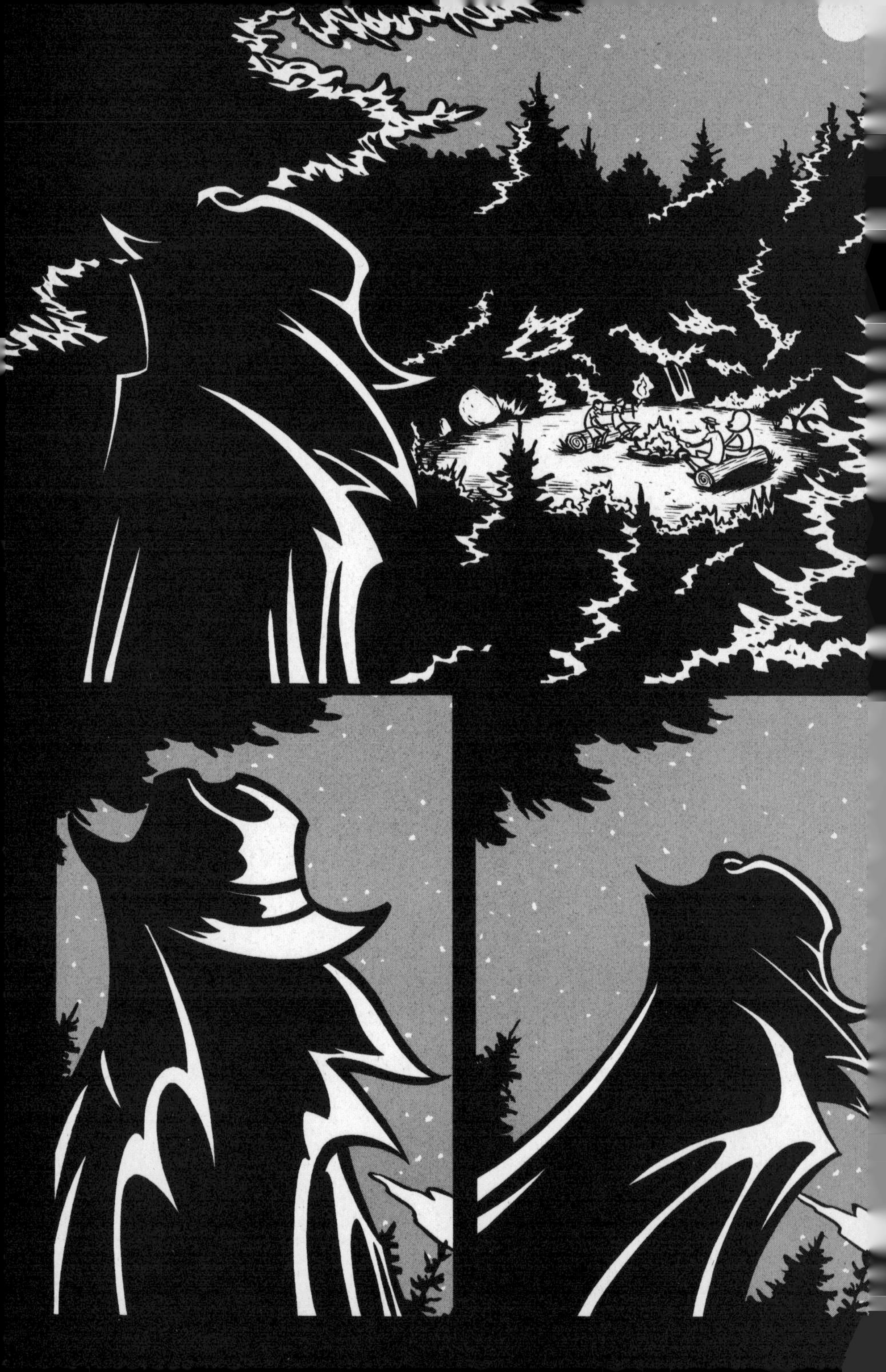

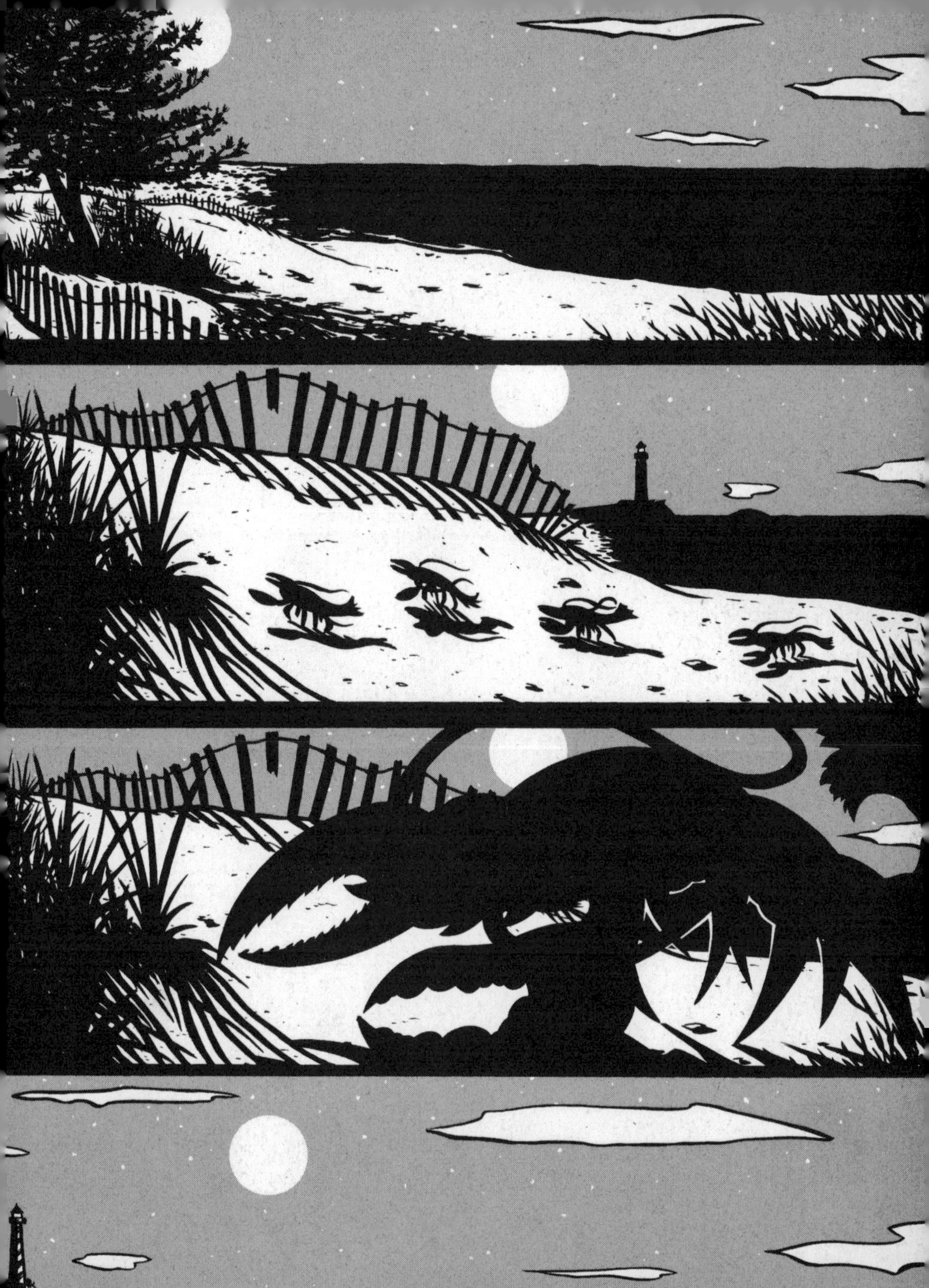

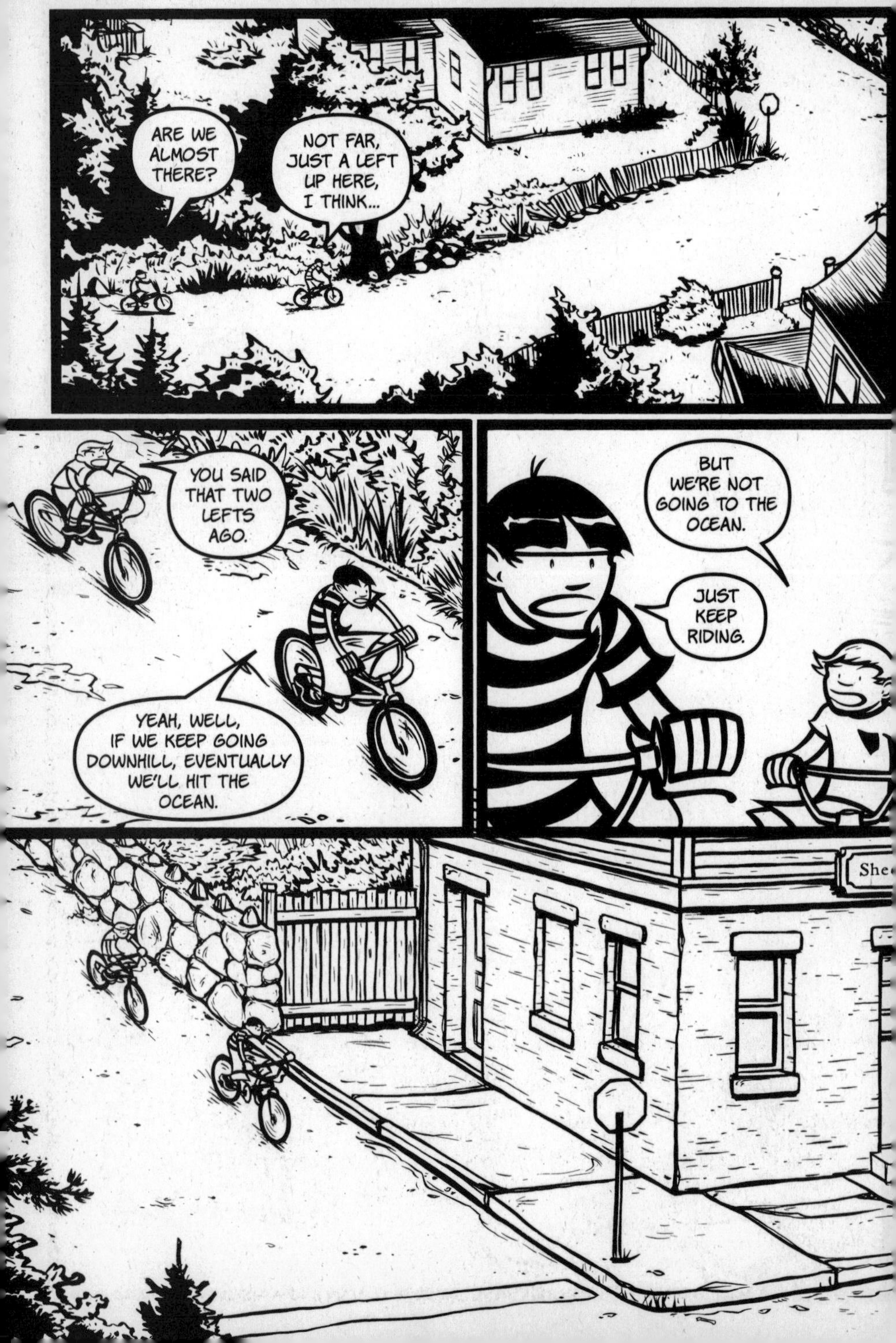
ARE WE ALMOST THERE?
NOT FAR, JUST A LEFT UP HERE, I THINK...
YOU SAID THAT TWO LEFTS AGO.
YEAH, WELL, IF WE KEEP GOING DOWNHILL, EVENTUALLY WE'LL HIT THE OCEAN.
BUT WE'RE NOT GOING TO THE OCEAN.
JUST KEEP RIDING.

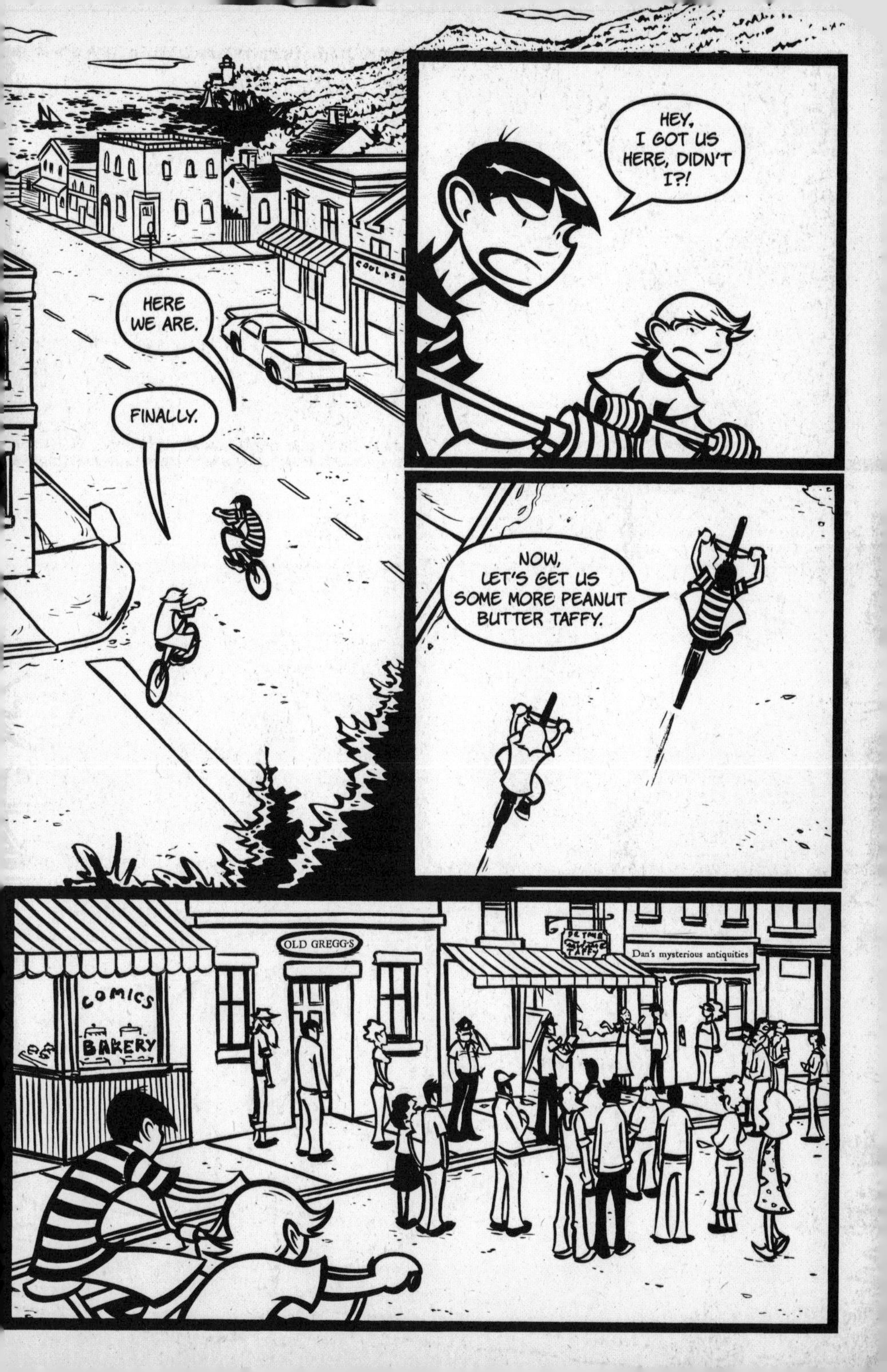
HERE WE ARE.
FINALLY.
HEY, I GOT US HERE, DIDN'T I?!
NOW, LET'S GET US SOME MORE PEANUT BUTTER TAFFY.
COMICS
BAKERY
OLD GREGG'S
Dan's mysterious antiquities

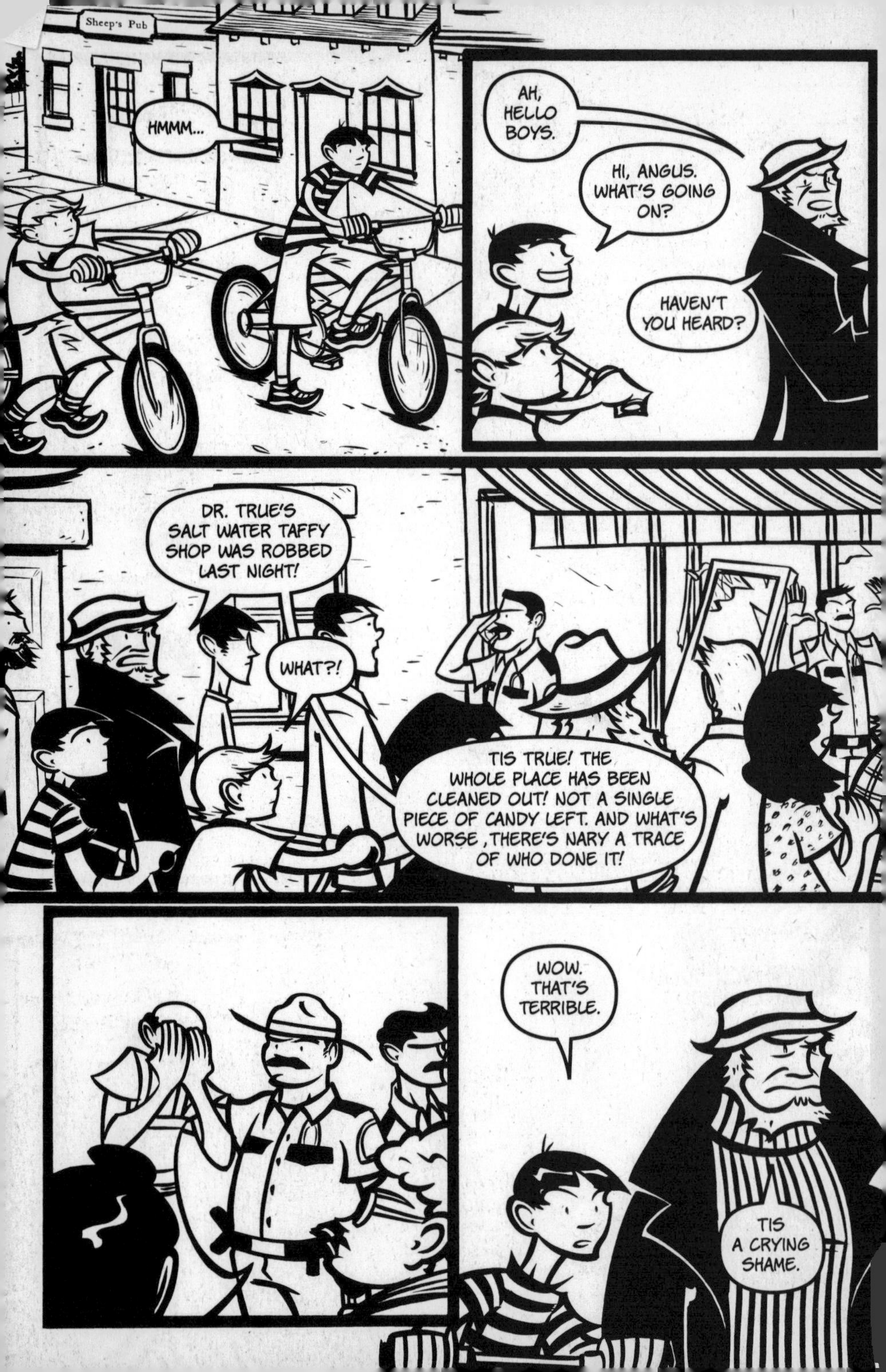
Sheep's Pub
HMMM...
AH, HELLO BOYS.
HI, ANGUS. WHAT'S GOING ON?
HAVEN'T YOU HEARD?
DR. TRUE'S SALT WATER TAFFY SHOP WAS ROBBED LAST NIGHT!
WHAT?!
TIS TRUE! THE WHOLE PLACE HAS BEEN CLEANED OUT! NOT A SINGLE PIECE OF CANDY LEFT. AND WHAT'S WORSE, THERE'S NARY A TRACE OF WHO DONE IT!
WOW. THAT'S TERRIBLE.
TIS A CRYING SHAME.

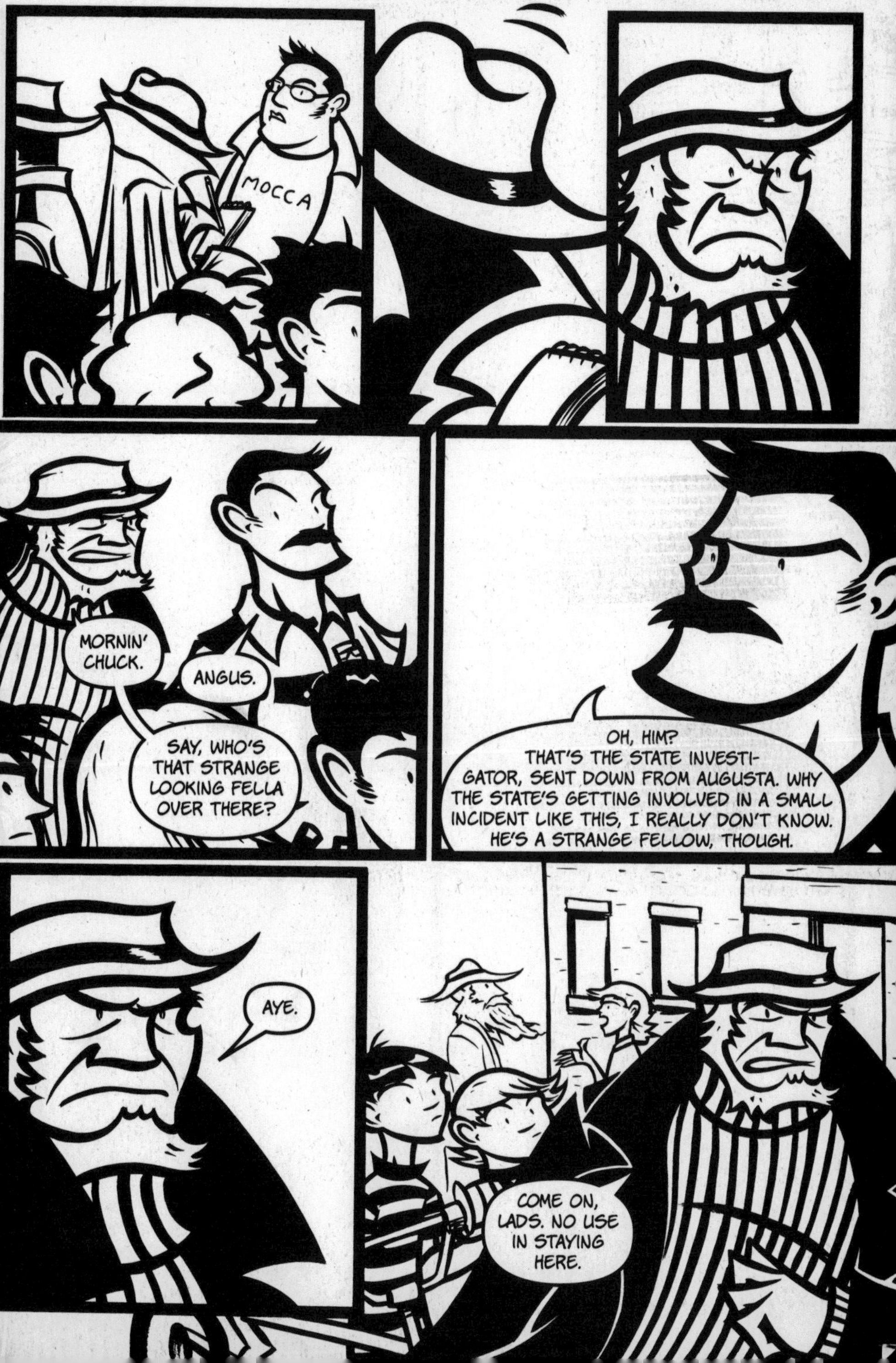
MOCCA
MORNIN' CHUCK.
ANGUS.
SAY, WHO'S THAT STRANGE LOOKING FELLA OVER THERE?
OH, HIM? THAT'S THE STATE INVESTI- GATOR, SENT DOWN FROM AUGUSTA. WHY THE STATE'S GETTING INVOLVED IN A SMALL INCIDENT LIKE THIS, I REALLY DON'T KNOW. HE'S A STRANGE FELLOW, THOUGH.
AYE.
COME ON, LADS. NO USE IN STAYING HERE.

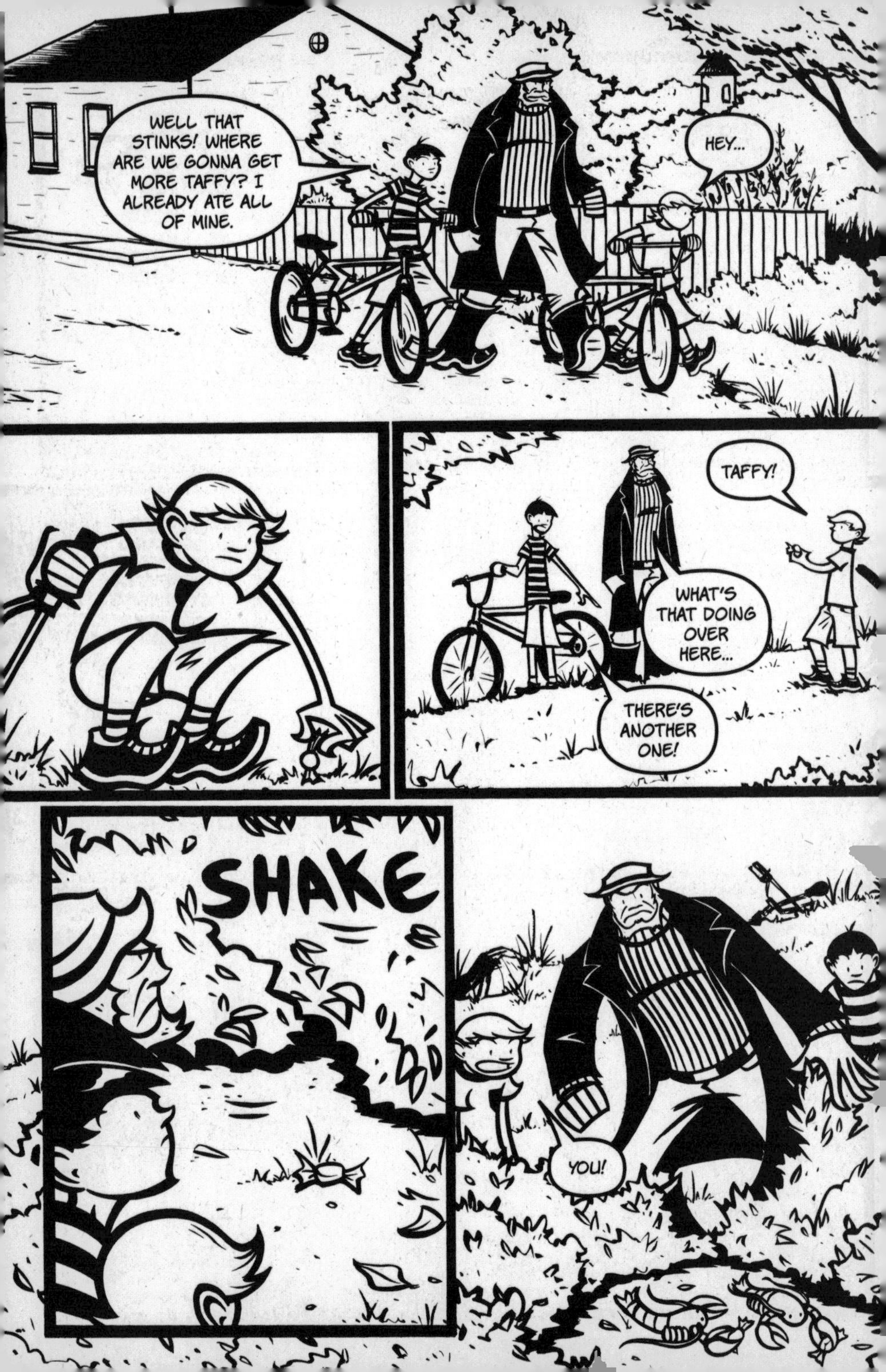
WELL THAT STINKS! WHERE ARE WE GONNA GET MORE TAFFY? I ALREADY ATE ALL OF MINE.
HEY...
TAFFY!
WHAT'S THAT DOING OVER HERE...
THERE'S ANOTHER ONE!
SHAKE
YOU!

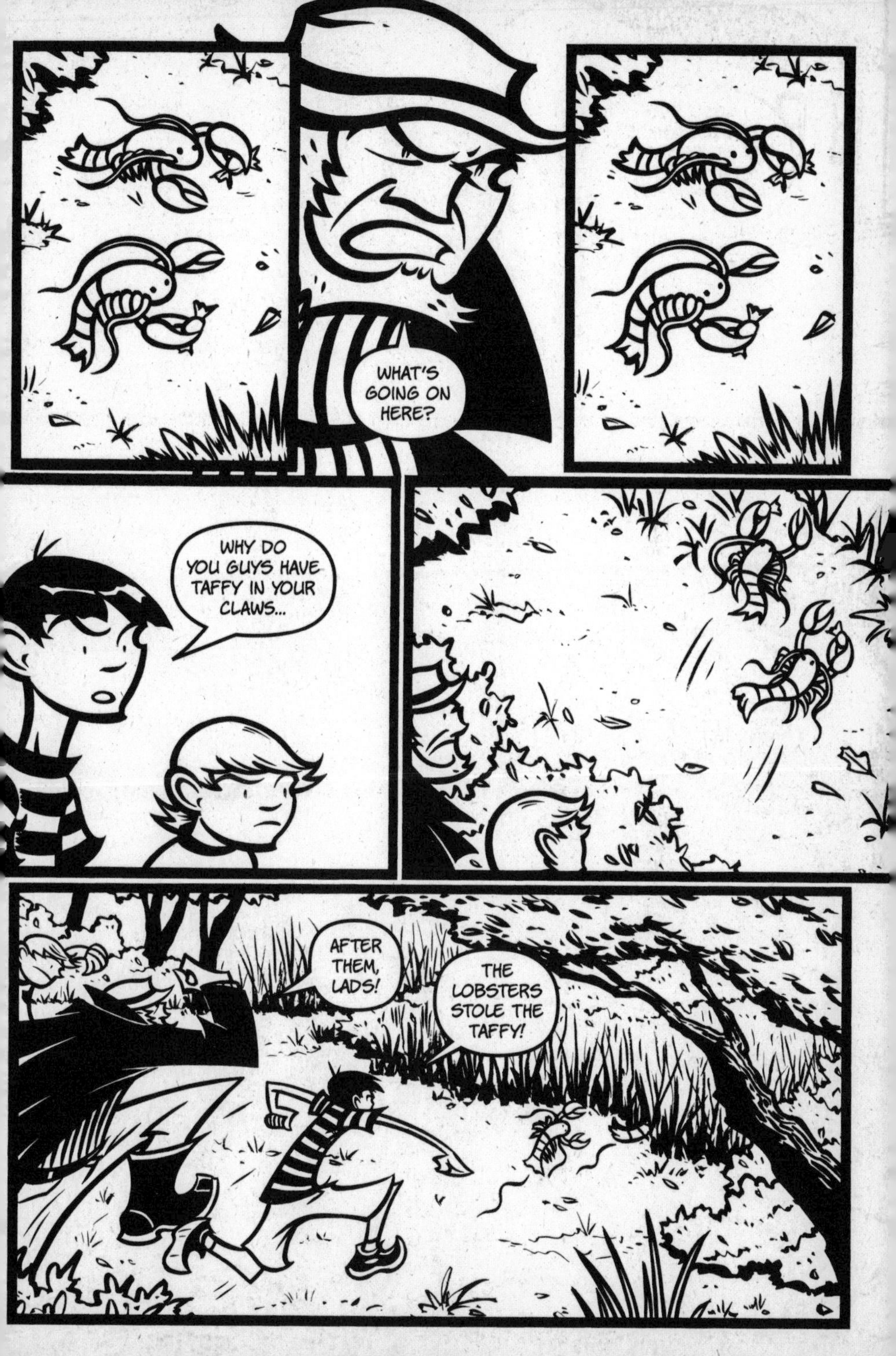
WHAT'S GOING ON HERE?
WHY DO YOU GUYS HAVE TAFFY IN YOUR CLAWS...
AFTER THEM, LADS!
THE LOBSTERS STOLE THE TAFFY!

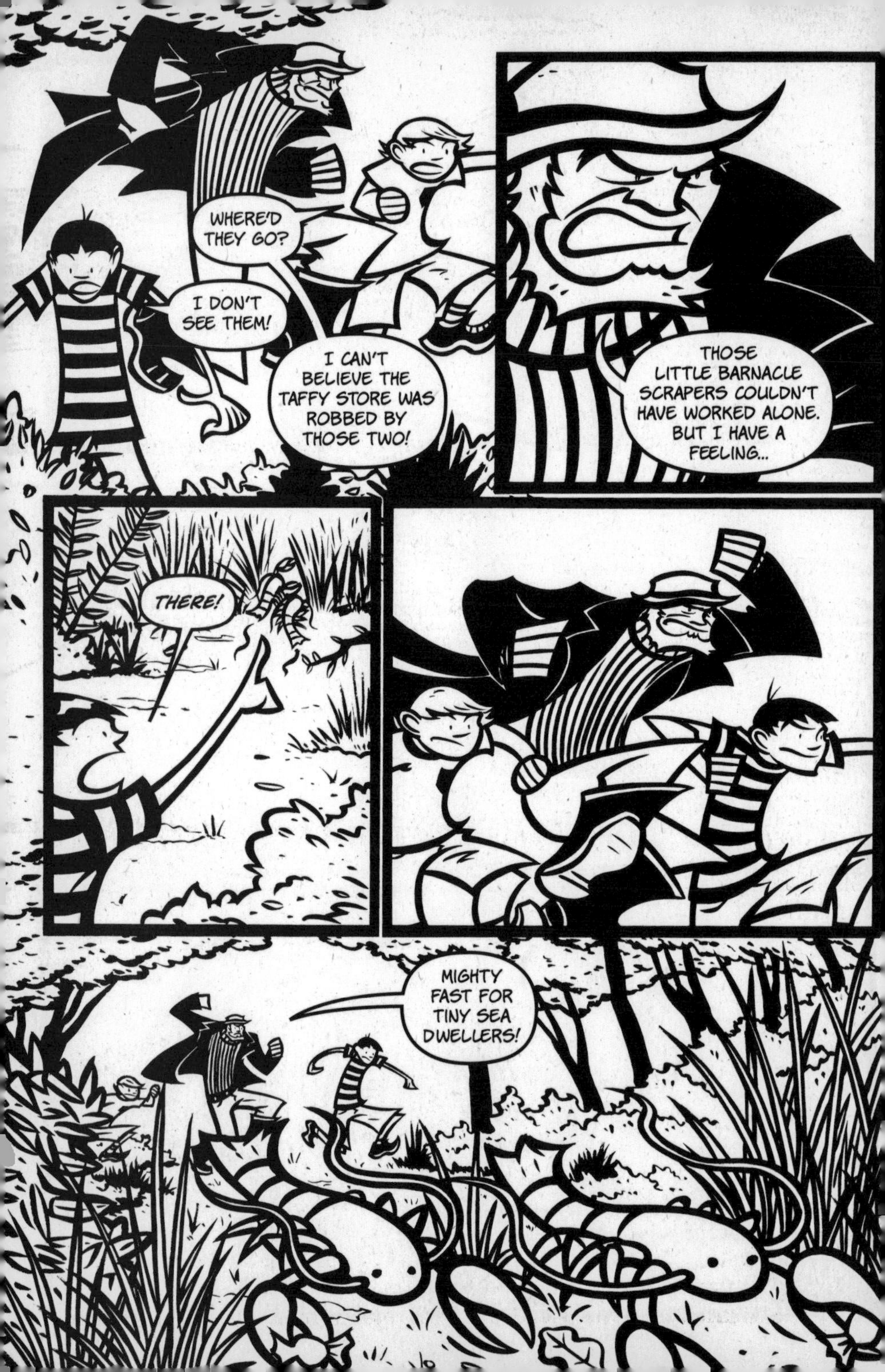
WHERE'D THEY GO?
I DON'T SEE THEM!
I CAN'T BELIEVE THE TAFFY STORE WAS ROBBED BY THOSE TWO!
THOSE LITTLE BARNACLE SCRAPERS COULDN'T HAVE WORKED ALONE. BUT I HAVE A FEELING...
THERE!
MIGHTY FAST FOR TINY SEA DWELLERS!

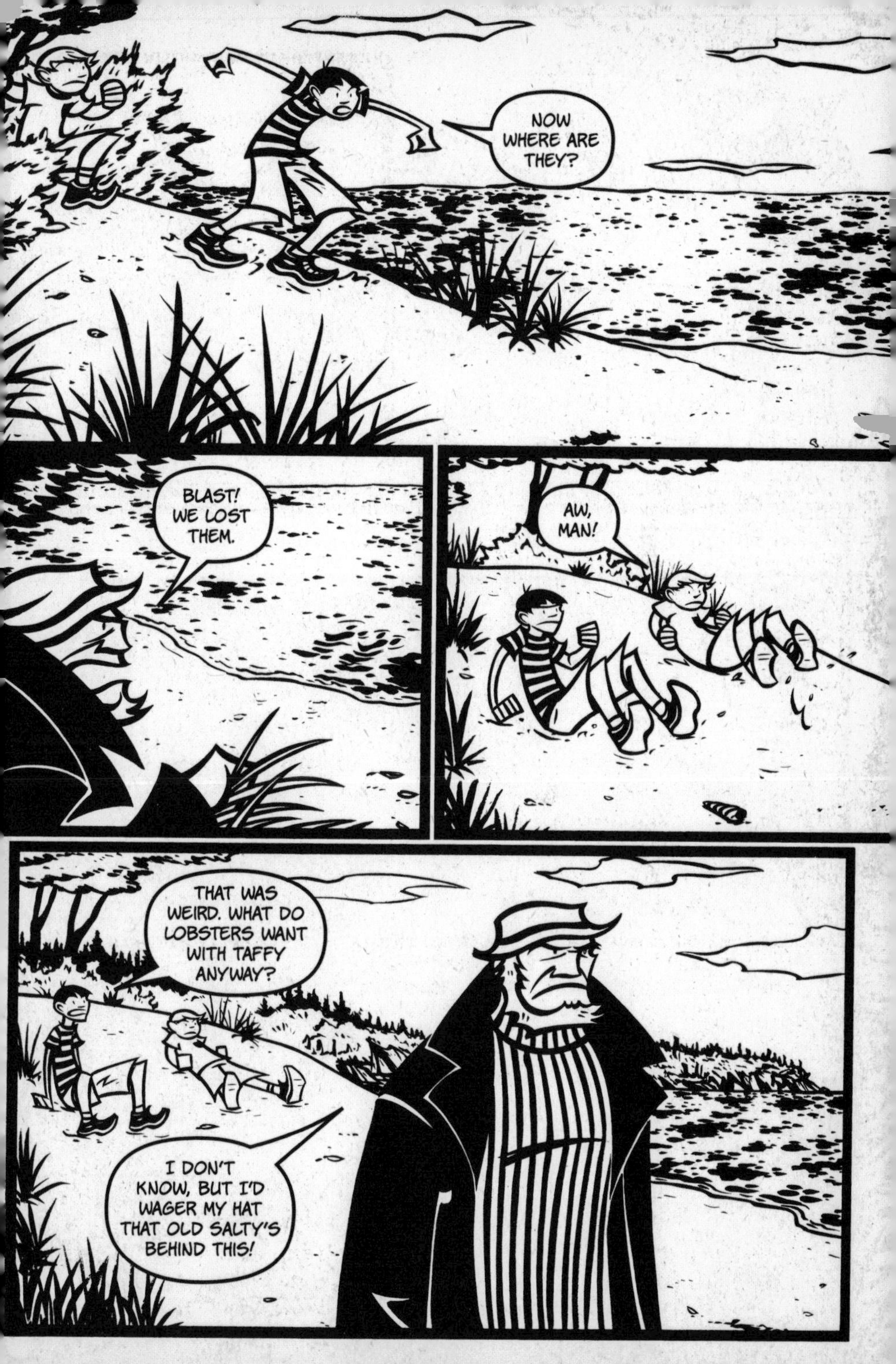
NOW WHERE ARE THEY?
BLAST! WE LOST THEM.
AW, MAN!
THAT WAS WEIRD. WHAT DO LOBSTERS WANT WITH TAFFY ANYWAY?
I DON'T KNOW, BUT I'D WAGER MY HAT THAT OLD SALTY'S BEHIND THIS!

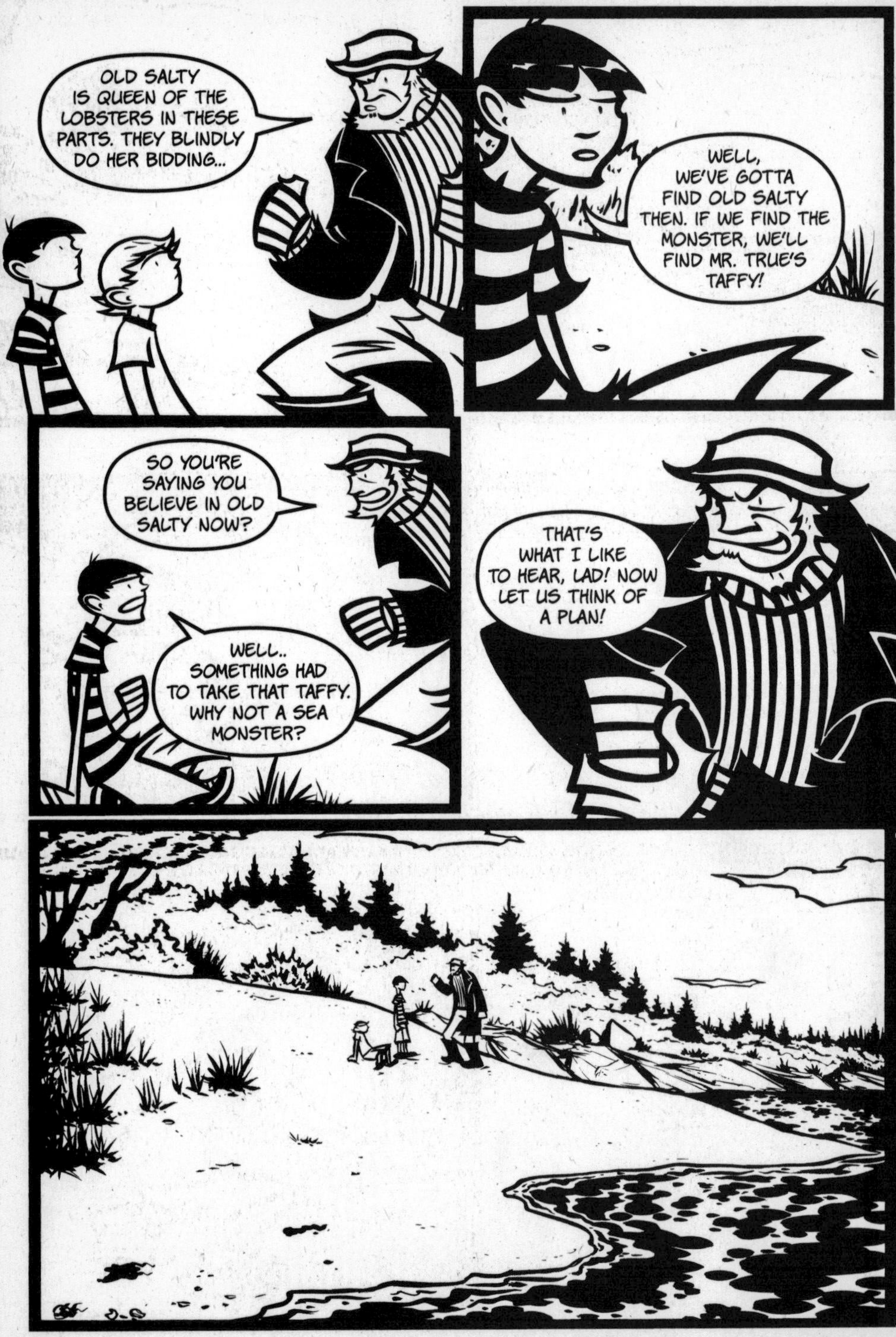
OLD SALTY IS QUEEN OF THE LOBSTERS IN THESE PARTS. THEY BLINDLY DO HER BIDDING...
WELL, WE'VE GOTTA FIND OLD SALTY THEN. IF WE FIND THE MONSTER, WE'LL FIND MR. TRUE'S TAFFY!
SO YOU'RE SAYING YOU BELIEVE IN OLD SALTY NOW?
WELL.. SOMETHING HAD TO TAKE THAT TAFFY. WHY NOT A SEA MONSTER?
THAT'S WHAT I LIKE TO HEAR, LAD! NOW LET US THINK OF A PLAN!

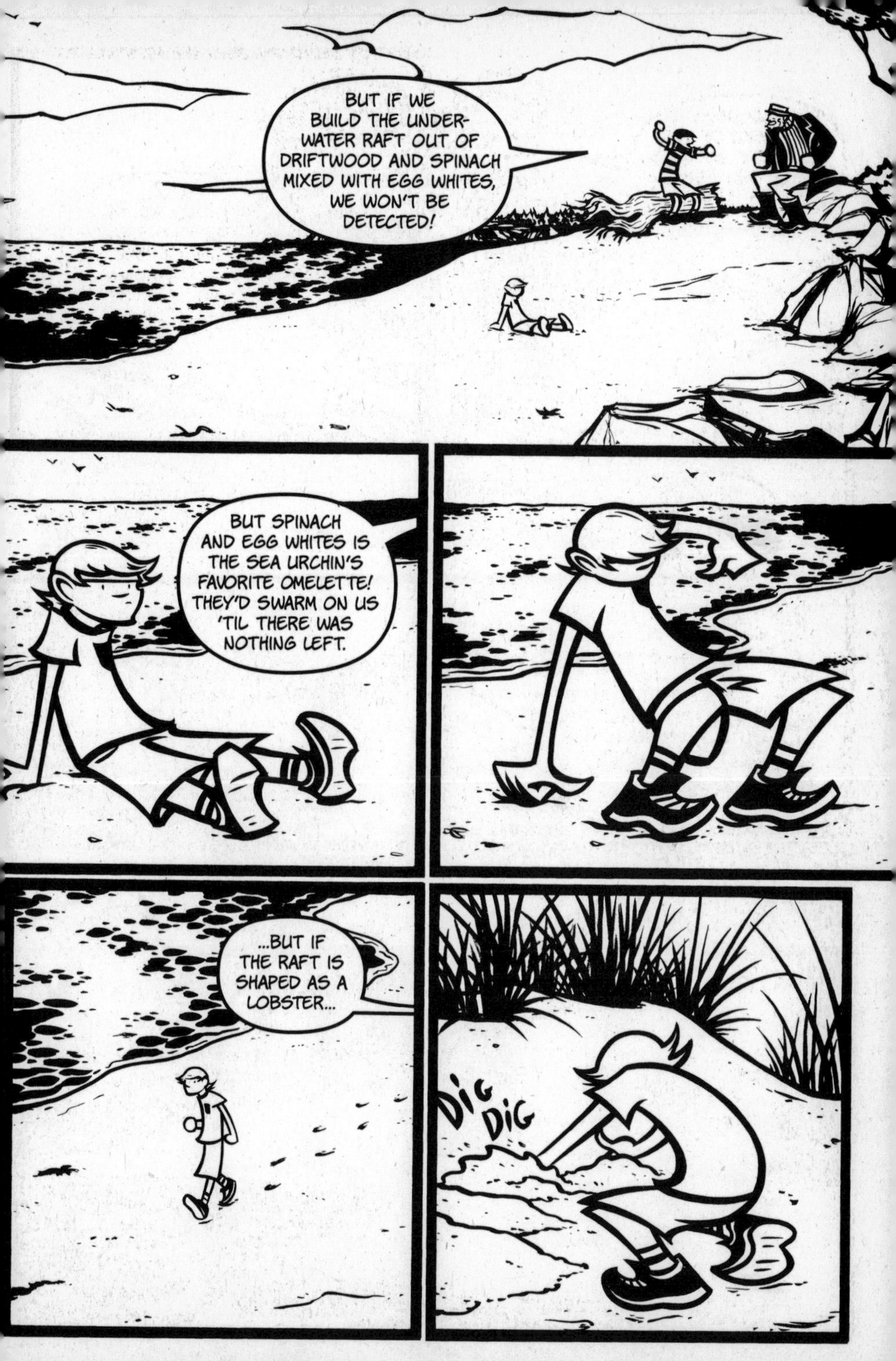
BUT IF WE BUILD THE UNDER-WATER RAFT OUT OF DRIFTWOOD AND SPINACH MIXED WITH EGG WHITES, WE WON'T BE DETECTED!
BUT SPINACH AND EGG WHITES IS THE SEA URCHIN'S FAVORITE OMELETTE! THEY'D SWARM ON US 'TIL THERE WAS NOTHING LEFT.
...BUT IF THE RAFT IS SHAPED AS A LOBSTER...
DIG
DIG

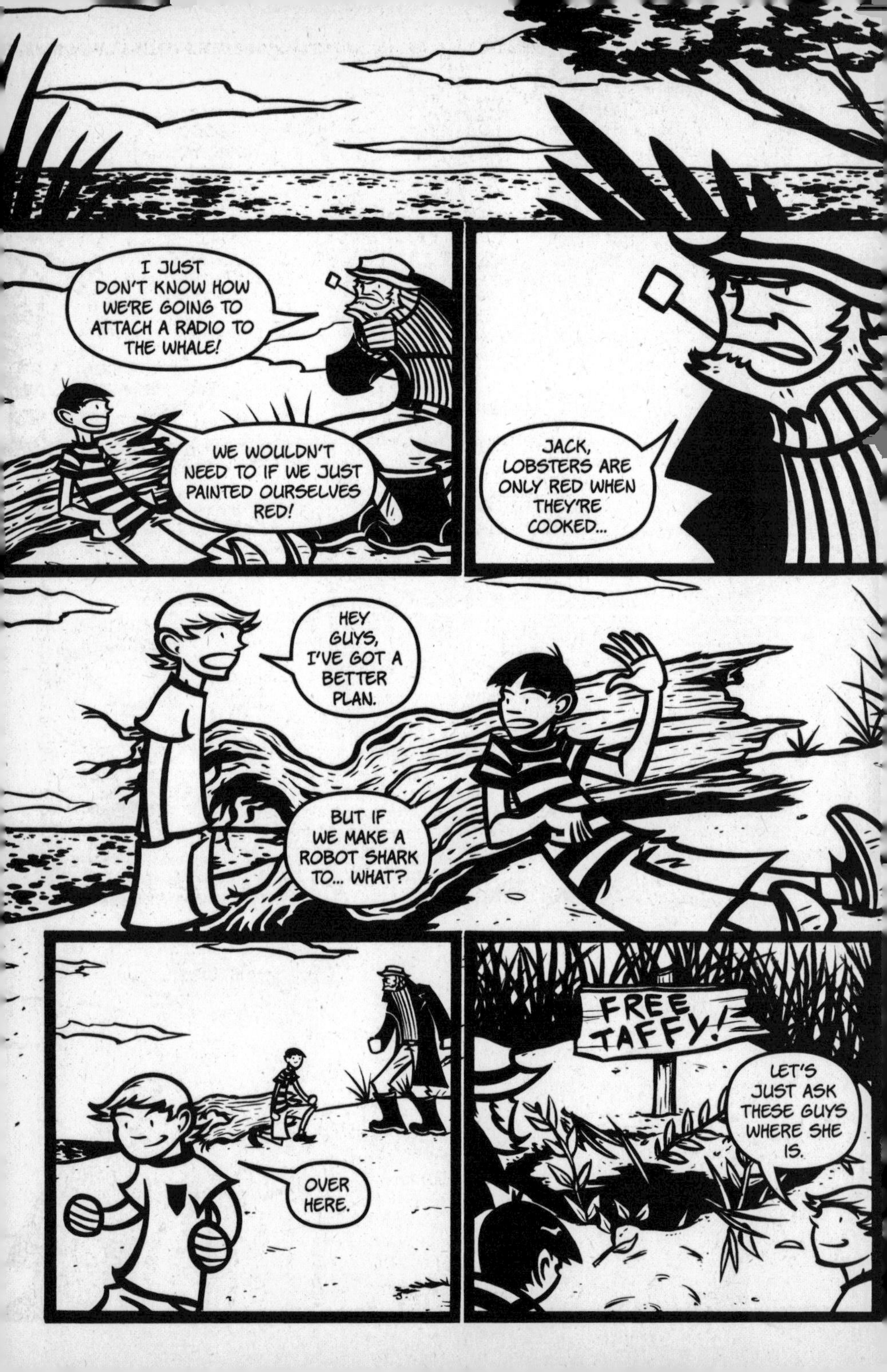
I JUST DON'T KNOW HOW WE'RE GOING TO ATTACH A RADIO TO THE WHALE!
WE WOULDN'T NEED TO IF WE JUST PAINTED OURSELVES RED!
JACK, LOBSTERS ARE ONLY RED WHEN THEY'RE COOKED...
HEY GUYS, I'VE GOT A BETTER PLAN.
BUT IF WE MAKE A ROBOT SHARK TO... WHAT?
OVER HERE.
FREE TAFFY!
LET'S JUST ASK THESE GUYS WHERE SHE IS.

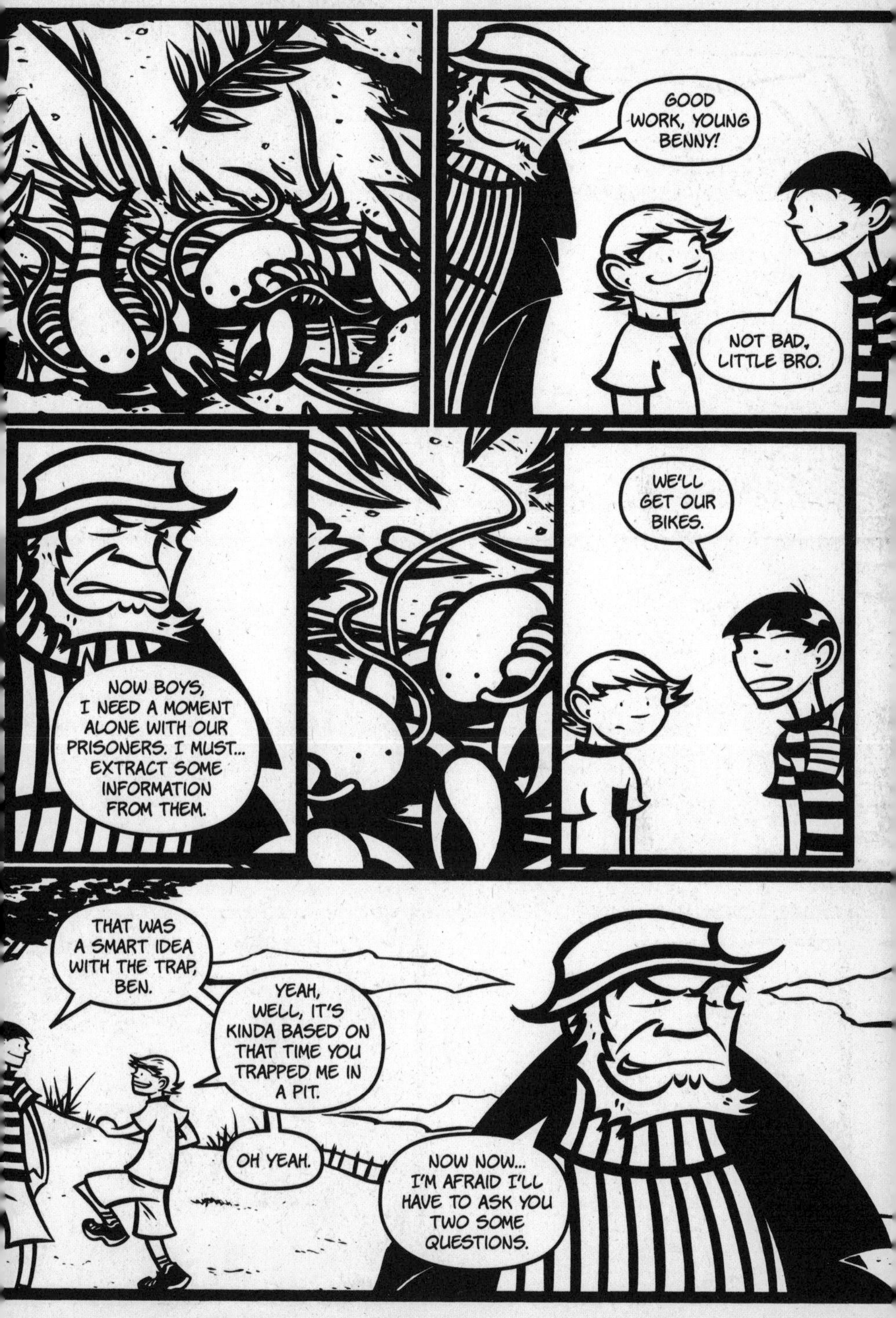
GOOD WORK, YOUNG BENNY!
NOT BAD, LITTLE BRO.
NOW BOYS, I NEED A MOMENT ALONE WITH OUR PRISONERS. I MUST... EXTRACT SOME INFORMATION FROM THEM.
WE'LL GET OUR BIKES.
THAT WAS A SMART IDEA WITH THE TRAP, BEN.
YEAH, WELL, IT'S KINDA BASED ON THAT TIME YOU TRAPPED ME IN A PIT.
OH YEAH.
NOW NOW... I'M AFRAID I'LL HAVE TO ASK YOU TWO SOME QUESTIONS.

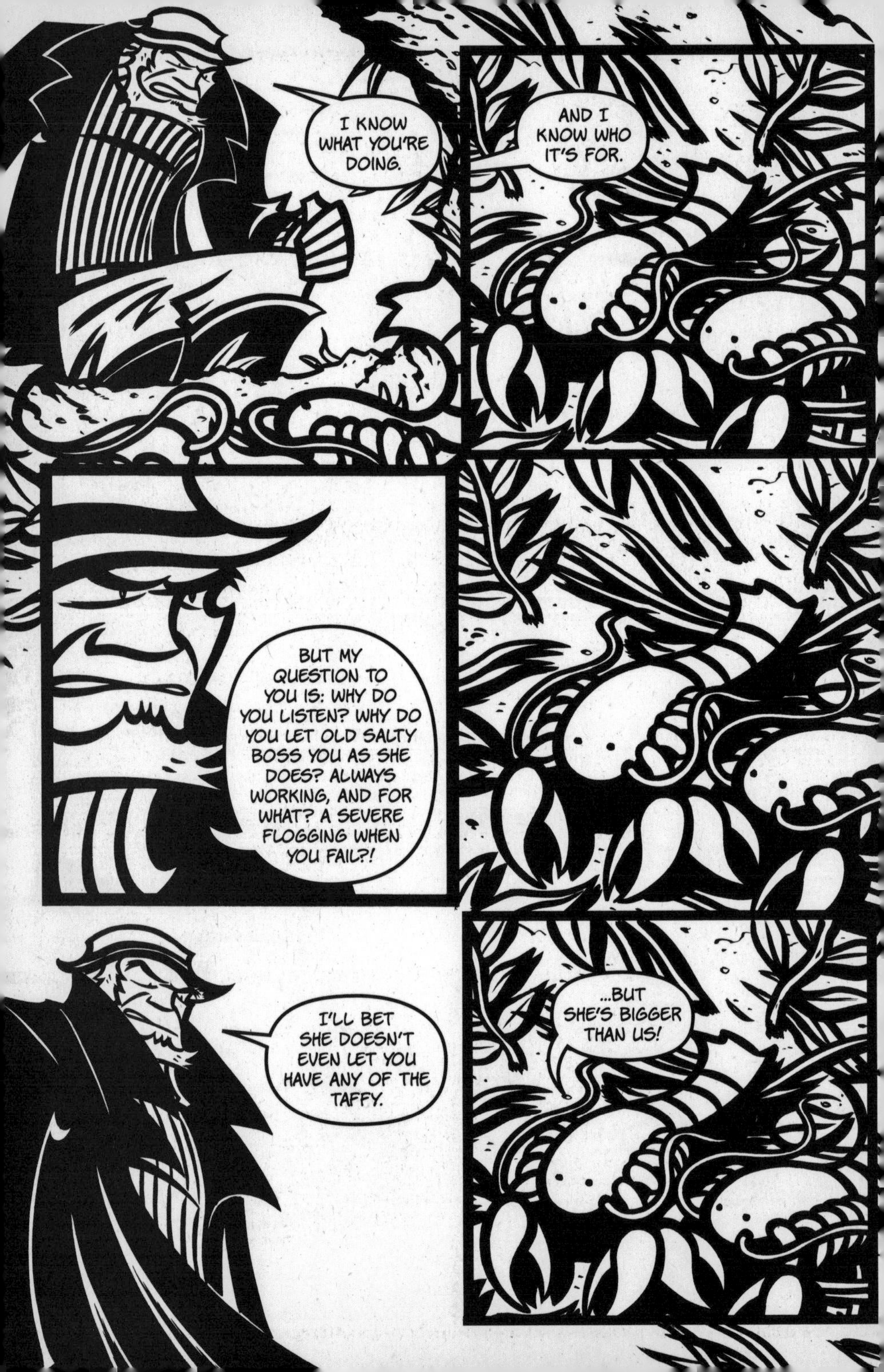
I KNOW WHAT YOU'RE DOING.
AND I KNOW WHO IT'S FOR.
BUT MY QUESTION TO YOU IS: WHY DO YOU LISTEN? WHY DO YOU LET OLD SALTY BOSS YOU AS SHE DOES? ALWAYS WORKING, AND FOR WHAT? A SEVERE FLOGGING WHEN YOU FAIL?!
I'LL BET SHE DOESN'T EVEN LET YOU HAVE ANY OF THE TAFFY.
...BUT SHE'S BIGGER THAN US!

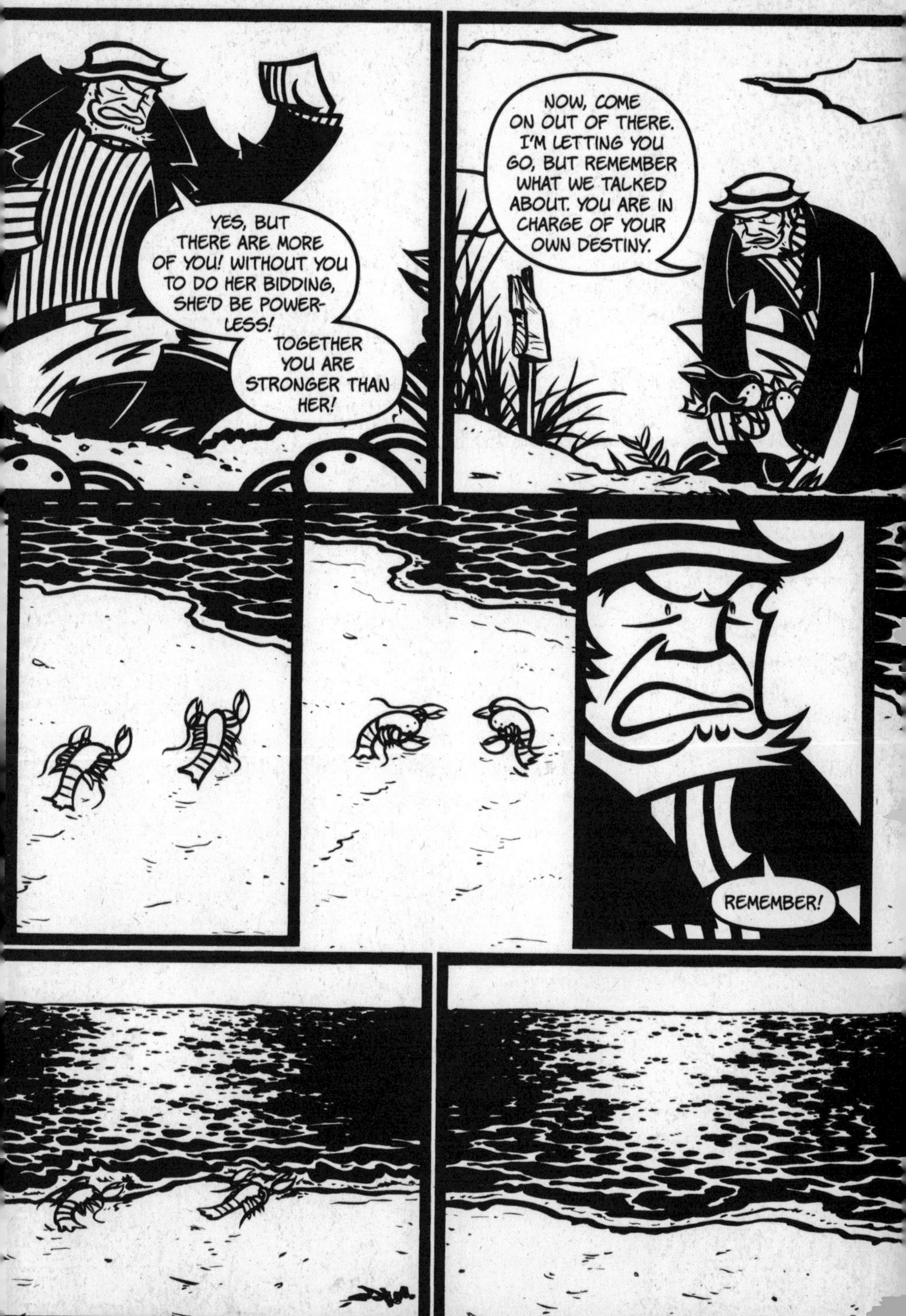
YES, BUT THERE ARE MORE OF YOU! WITHOUT YOU TO DO HER BIDDING, SHE'D BE POWER-LESS!
TOGETHER YOU ARE STRONGER THAN HER!
NOW, COME ON OUT OF THERE. I'M LETTING YOU GO, BUT REMEMBER WHAT WE TALKED ABOUT. YOU ARE IN CHARGE OF YOUR OWN DESTINY.
REMEMBER!

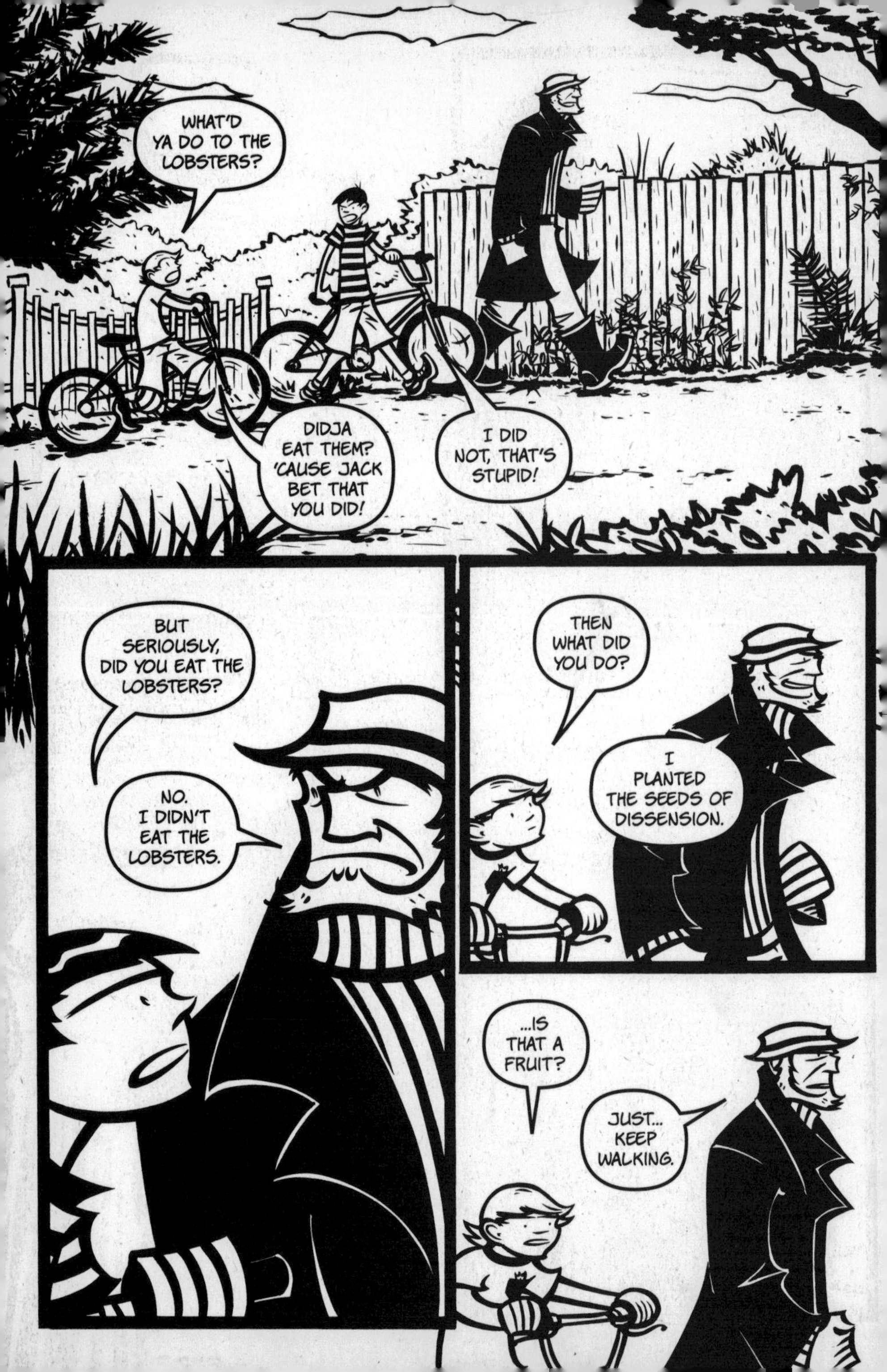
WHAT'D YA DO TO THE LOBSTERS?
DIDJA EAT THEM? 'CAUSE JACK BET THAT YOU DID!
I DID NOT, THAT'S STUPID!
BUT SERIOUSLY, DID YOU EAT THE LOBSTERS?
NO. I DIDN'T EAT THE LOBSTERS.
THEN WHAT DID YOU DO?
I PLANTED THE SEEDS OF DISSENSION.
...IS THAT A FRUIT?
JUST... KEEP WALKING.

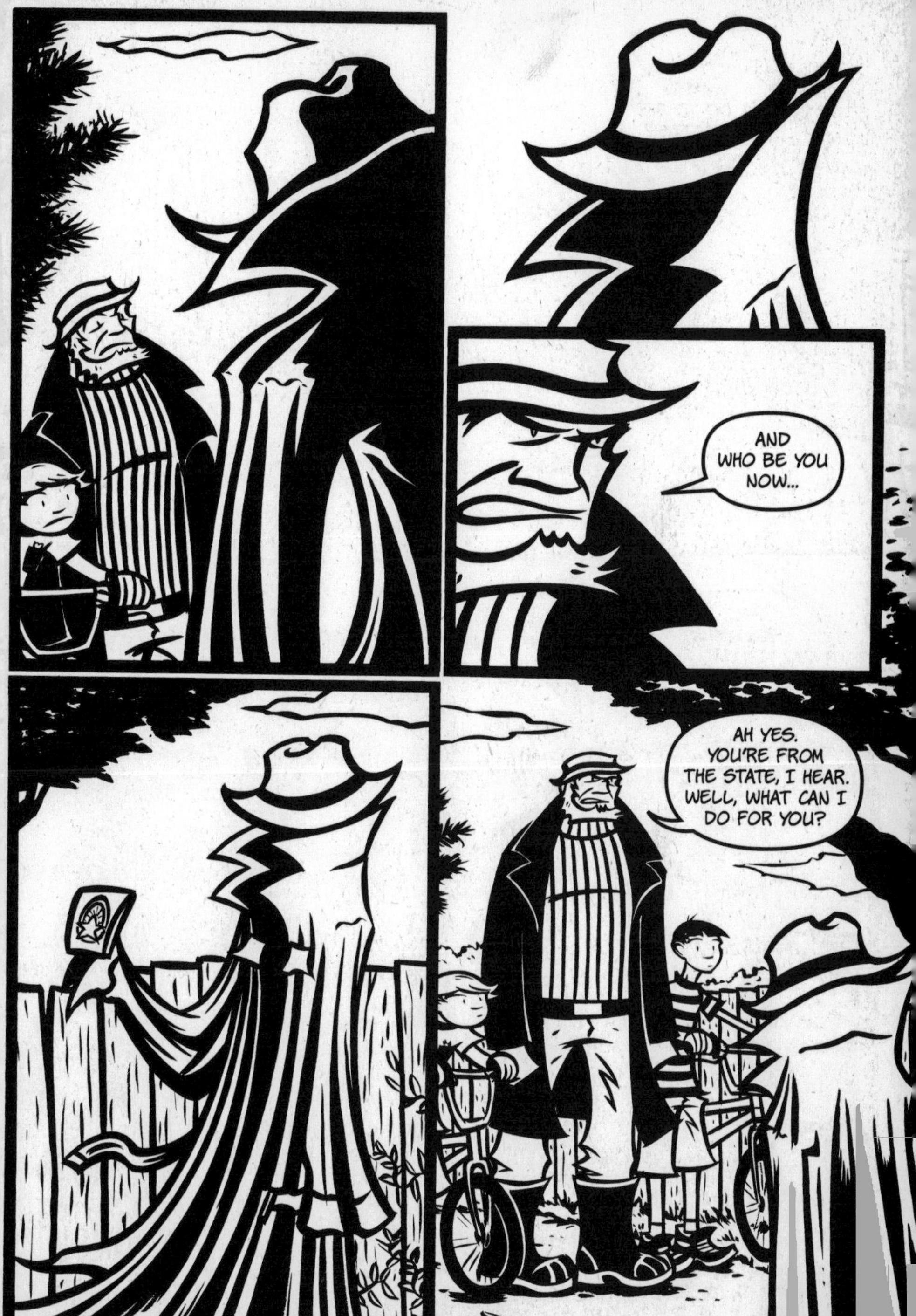
AND WHO BE YOU NOW...
AH YES. YOU'RE FROM THE STATE, I HEAR. WELL, WHAT CAN I DO FOR YOU?

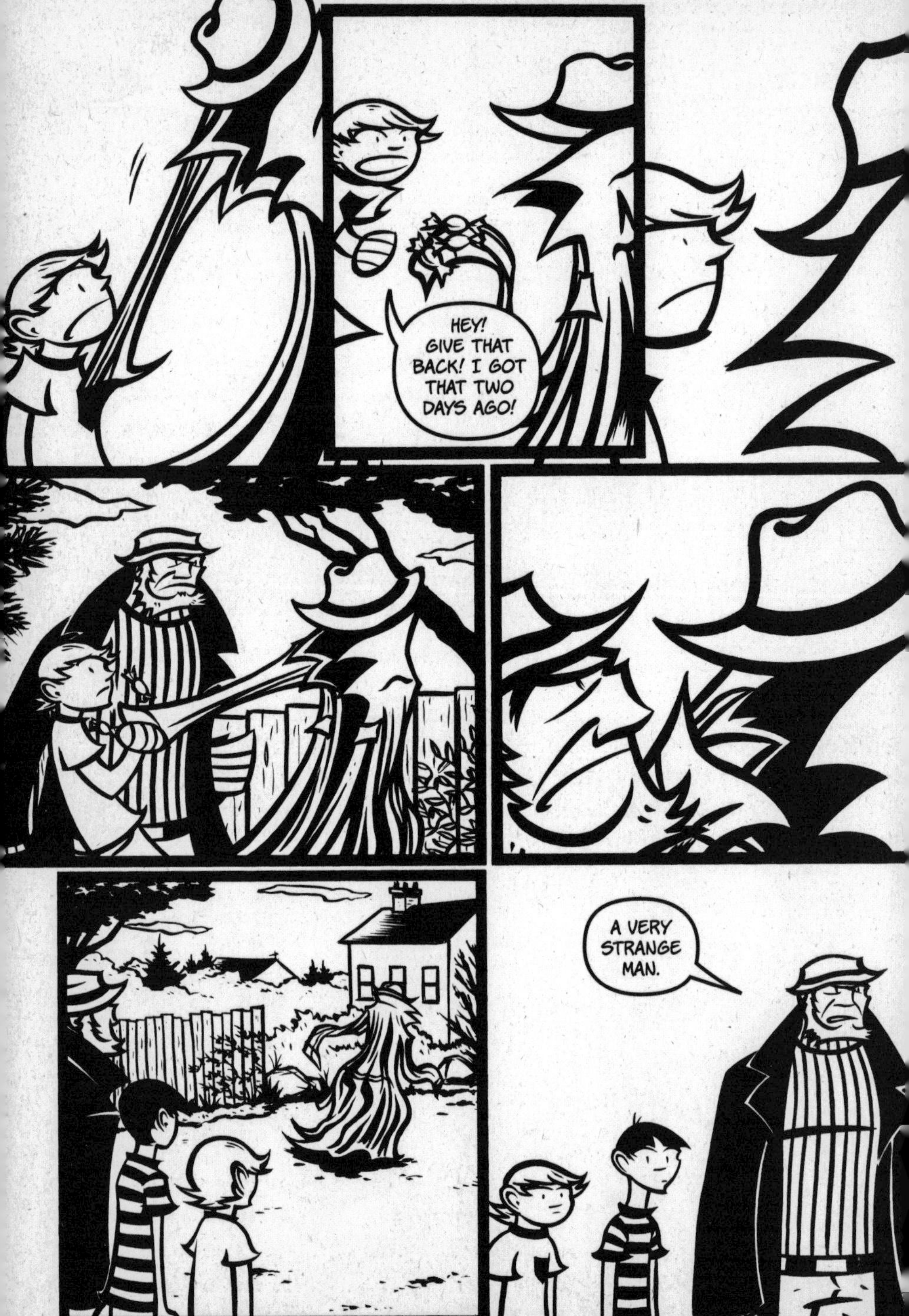
HEY! GIVE THAT BACK! I GOT THAT TWO DAYS AGO!
A VERY STRANGE MAN.

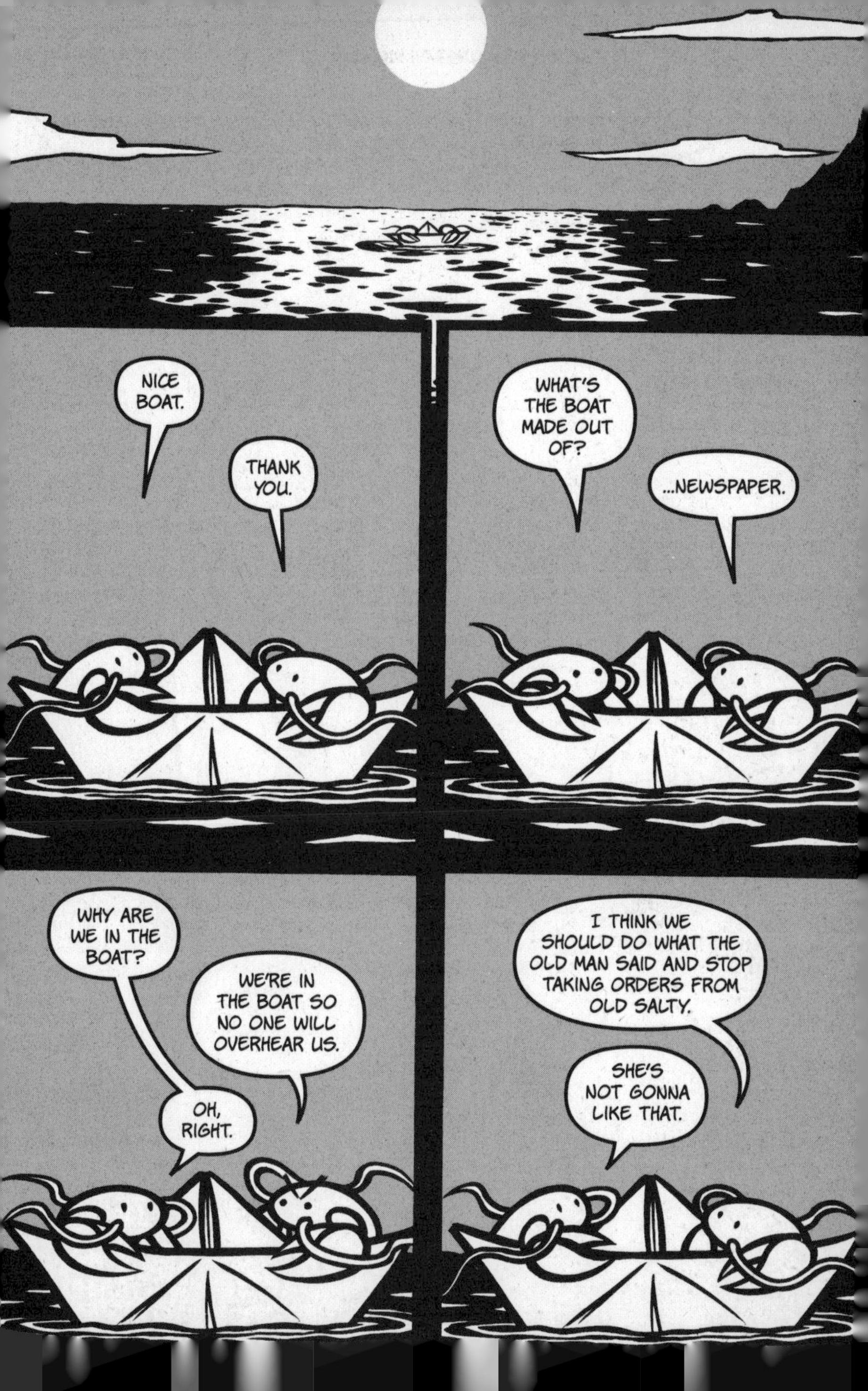
NICE BOAT.
THANK YOU.
WHAT'S THE BOAT MADE OUT OF?
...NEWSPAPER.
WHY ARE WE IN THE BOAT?
WE'RE IN THE BOAT SO NO ONE WILL OVERHEAR US.
OH, RIGHT.
I THINK WE SHOULD DO WHAT THE OLD MAN SAID AND STOP TAKING ORDERS FROM OLD SALTY.
SHE'S NOT GONNA LIKE THAT.

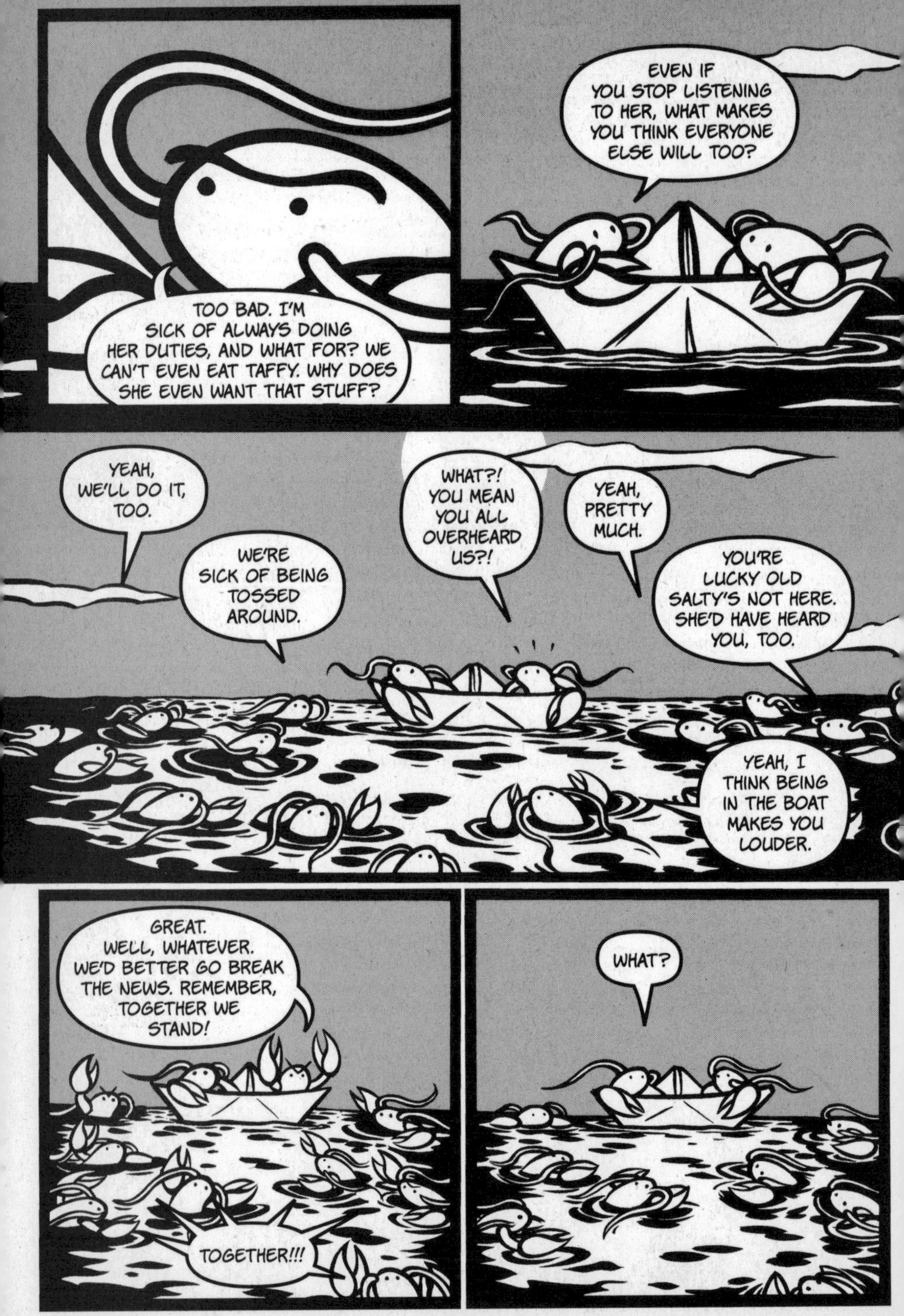
TOO BAD. I'M SICK OF ALWAYS DOING HER DUTIES, AND WHAT FOR? WE CAN'T EVEN EAT TAFFY. WHY DOES SHE EVEN WANT THAT STUFF?
EVEN IF YOU STOP LISTENING TO HER, WHAT MAKES YOU THINK EVERYONE ELSE WILL TOO?
YEAH, WE'LL DO IT, TOO.
WE'RE SICK OF BEING TOSSED AROUND.
WHAT?! YOU MEAN YOU ALL OVERHEARD US?!
YEAH, PRETTY MUCH.
YOU'RE LUCKY OLD SALTY'S NOT HERE. SHE'D HAVE HEARD YOU, TOO.
YEAH, I THINK BEING IN THE BOAT MAKES YOU LOUDER.
GREAT. WELL, WHATEVER. WE'D BETTER GO BREAK THE NEWS. REMEMBER, TOGETHER WE STAND!
TOGETHER!!!
WHAT?

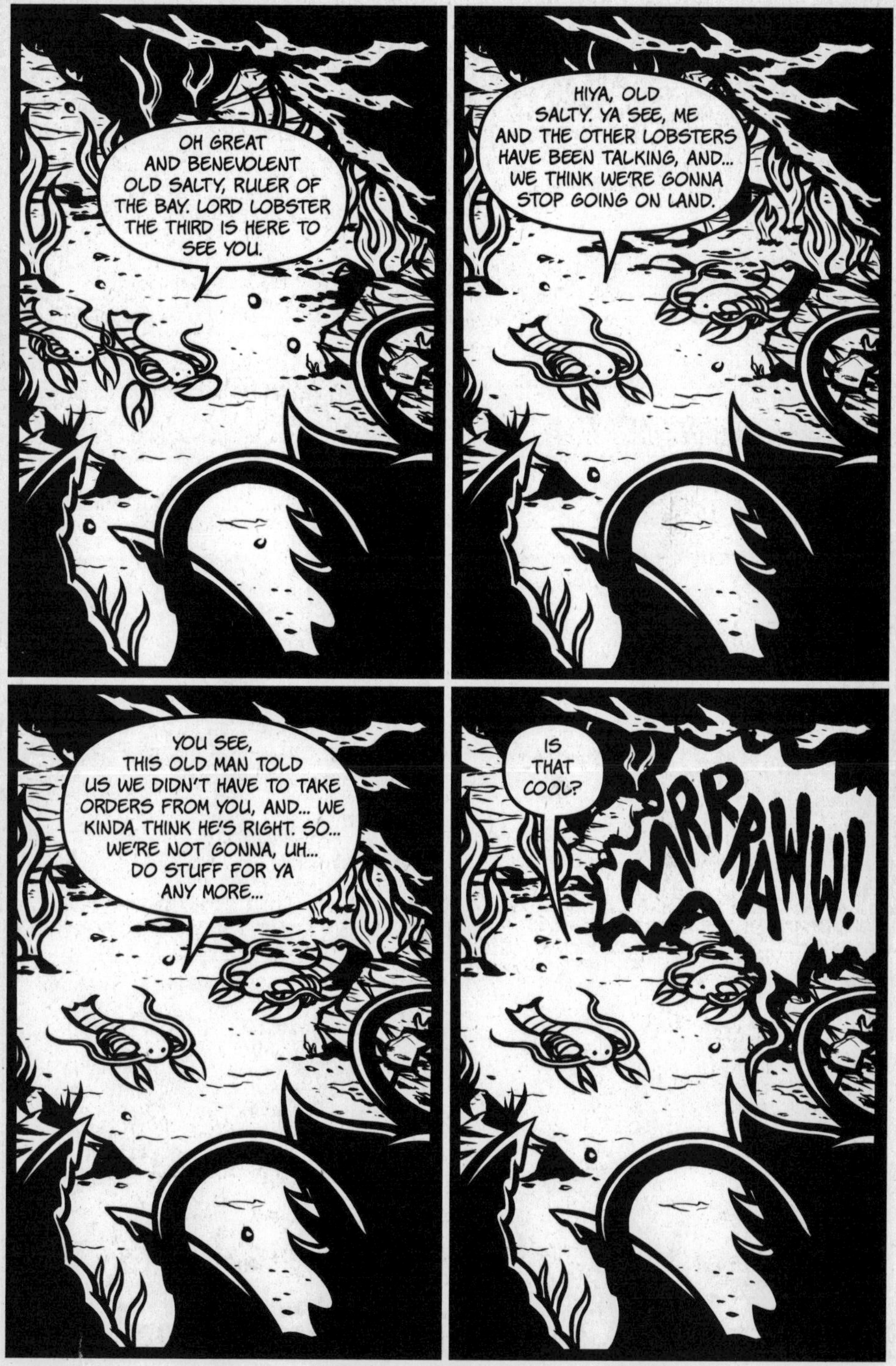
OH GREAT AND BENEVOLENT OLD SALTY, RULER OF THE BAY. LORD LOBSTER THE THIRD IS HERE TO SEE YOU.
HIYA, OLD SALTY. YA SEE, ME AND THE OTHER LOBSTERS HAVE BEEN TALKING, AND... WE THINK WE'RE GONNA STOP GOING ON LAND.
YOU SEE, THIS OLD MAN TOLD US WE DIDN'T HAVE TO TAKE ORDERS FROM YOU, AND... WE KINDA THINK HE'S RIGHT. SO... WE'RE NOT GONNA, UH... DO STUFF FOR YA ANY MORE...
IS THAT COOL?
MRRRAWW!

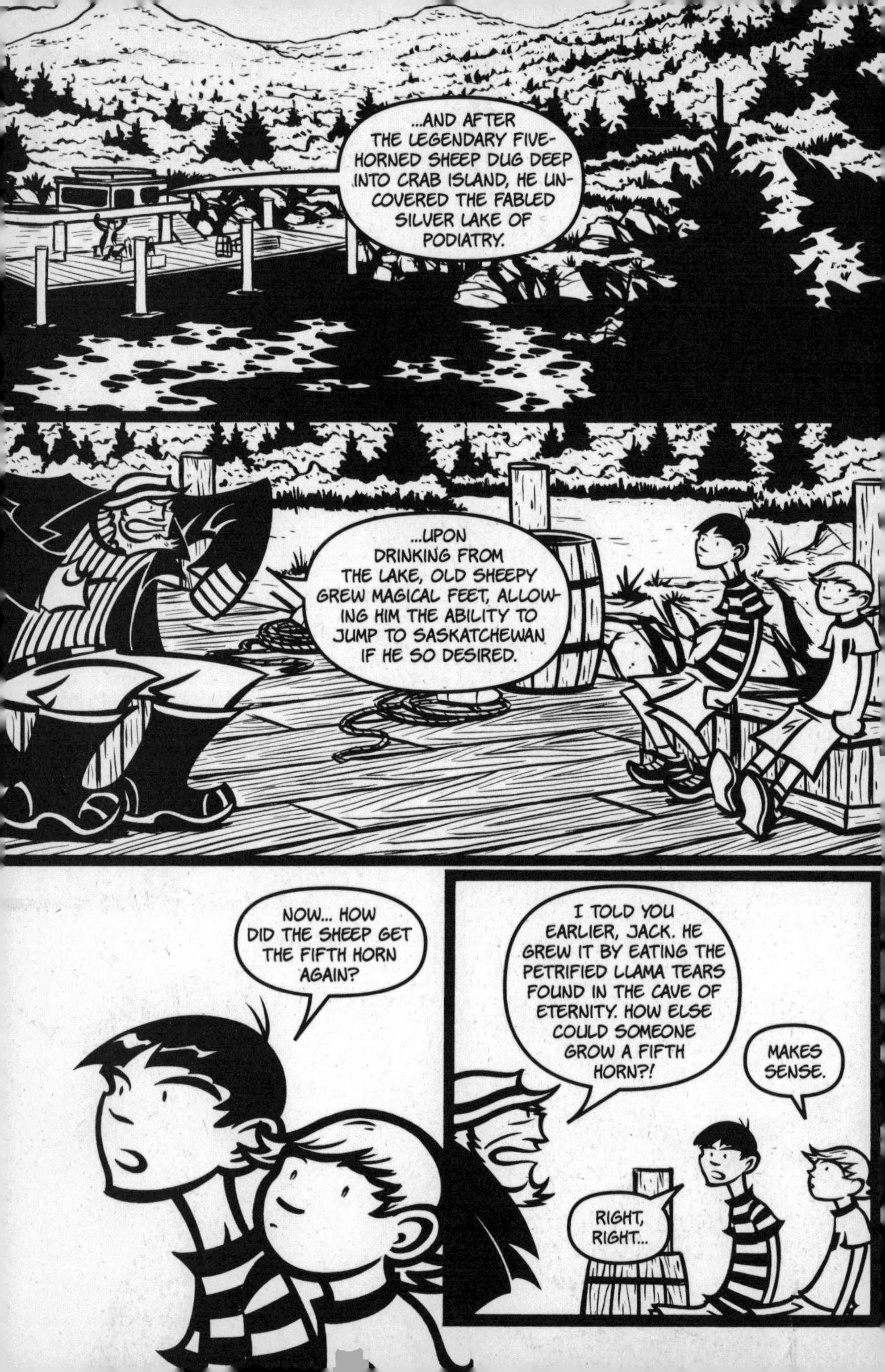
...AND AFTER THE LEGENDARY FIVE-HORNED SHEEP DUG DEEP INTO CRAB ISLAND, HE UNCOVERED THE FABLED SILVER LAKE OF PODIATRY.
...UPON DRINKING FROM THE LAKE, OLD SHEEPY GREW MAGICAL FEET, ALLOWING HIM THE ABILITY TO JUMP TO SASKATCHEWAN IF HE SO DESIRED.
NOW... HOW DID THE SHEEP GET THE FIFTH HORN AGAIN?
I TOLD YOU EARLIER, JACK. HE GREW IT BY EATING THE PETRIFIED LLAMA TEARS FOUND IN THE CAVE OF ETERNITY. HOW ELSE COULD SOMEONE GROW A FIFTH HORN?!
MAKES SENSE.
RIGHT, RIGHT...

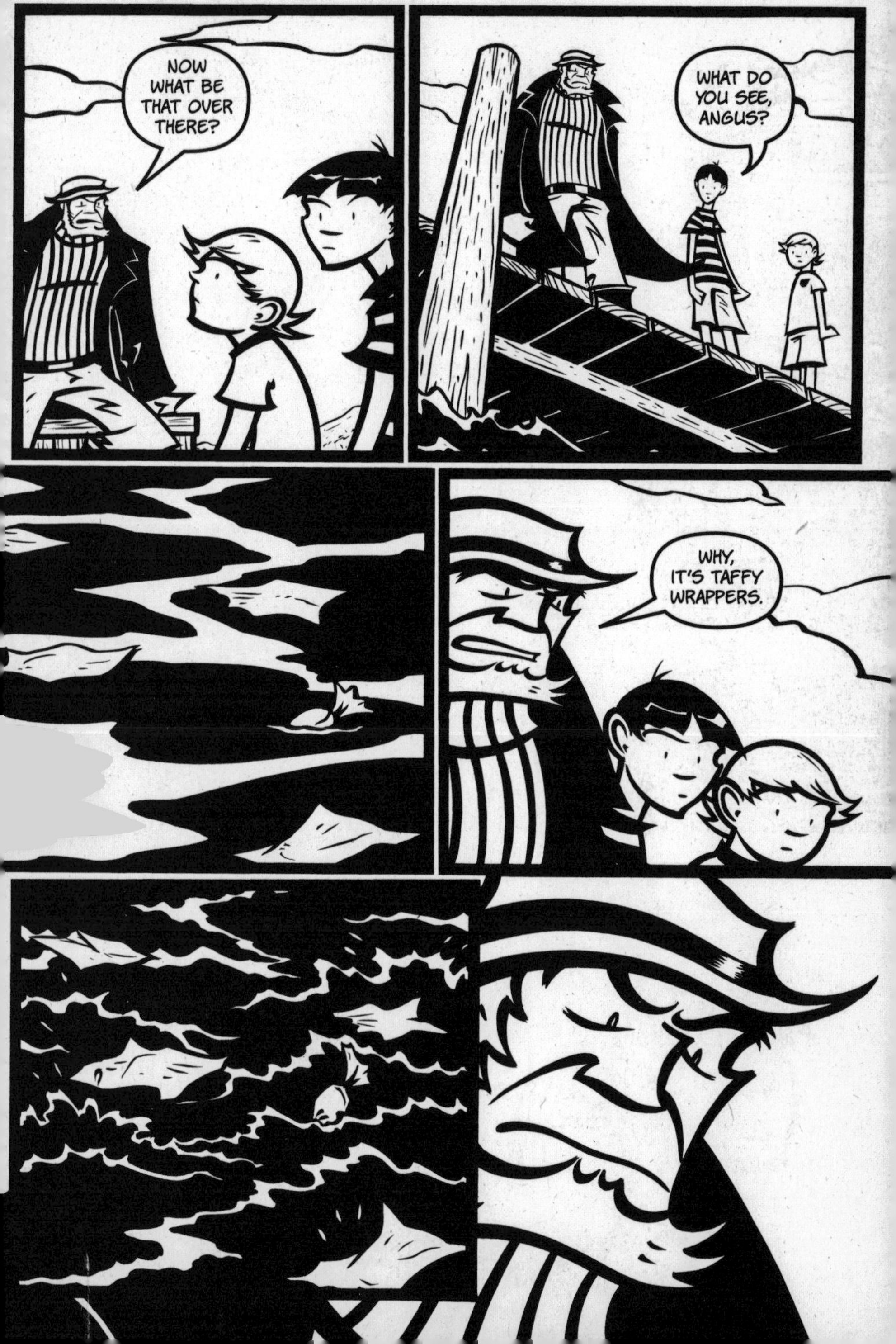
NOW WHAT BE THAT OVER THERE?
WHAT DO YOU SEE, ANGUS?
WHY, IT'S TAFFY WRAPPERS.

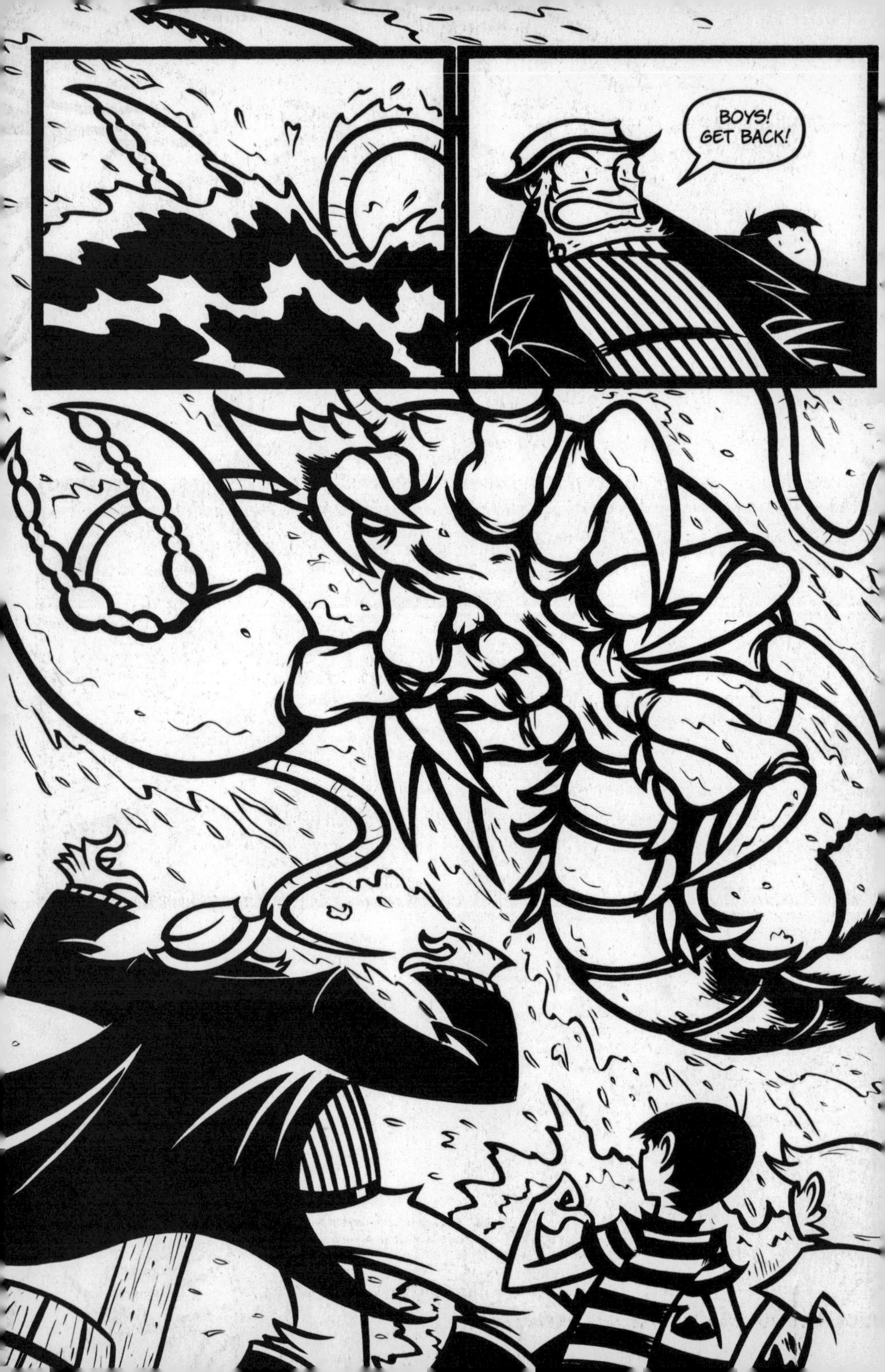
BOYS! GET BACK!

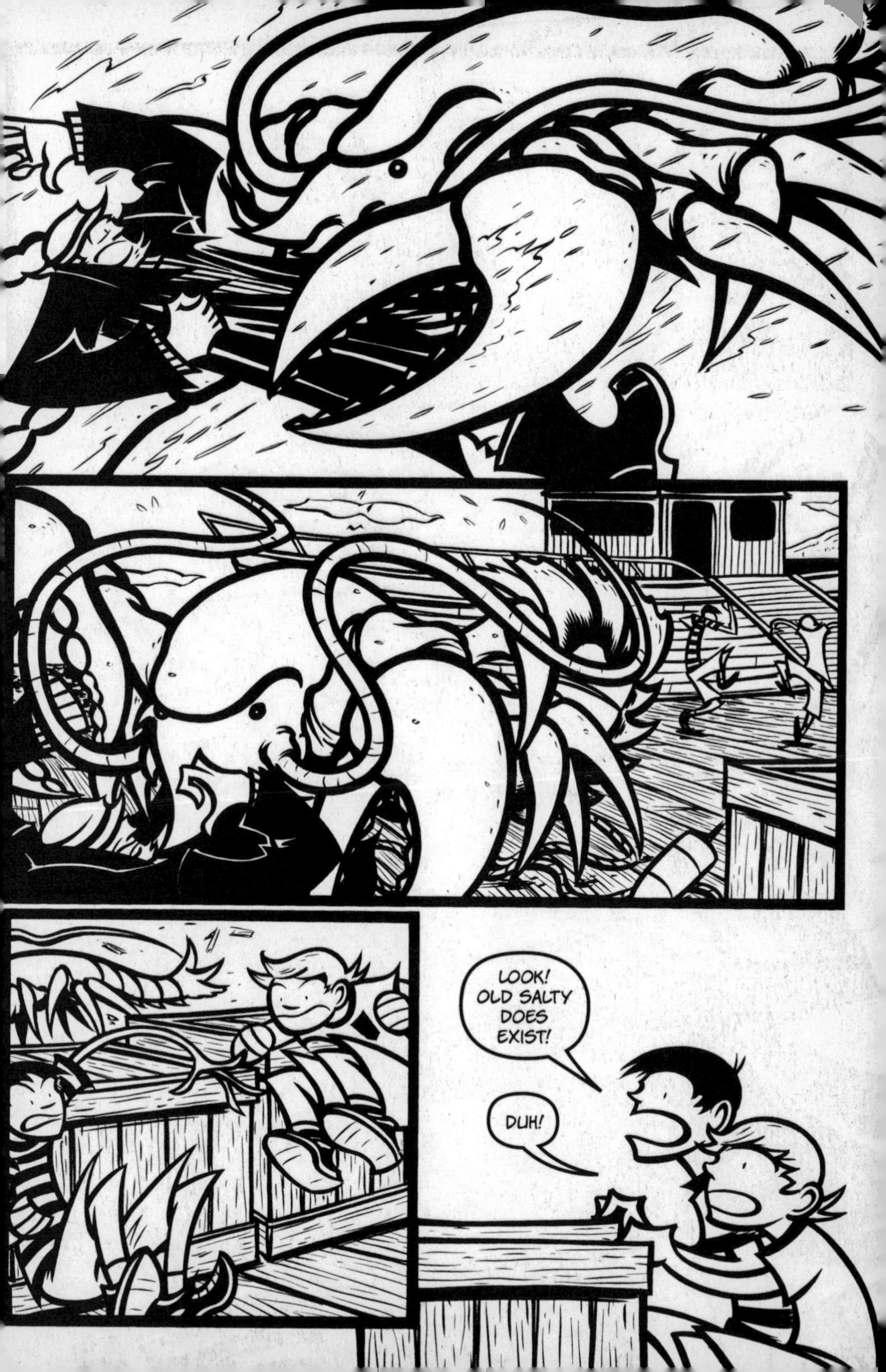
LOOK! OLD SALTY DOES EXIST!
DUH!

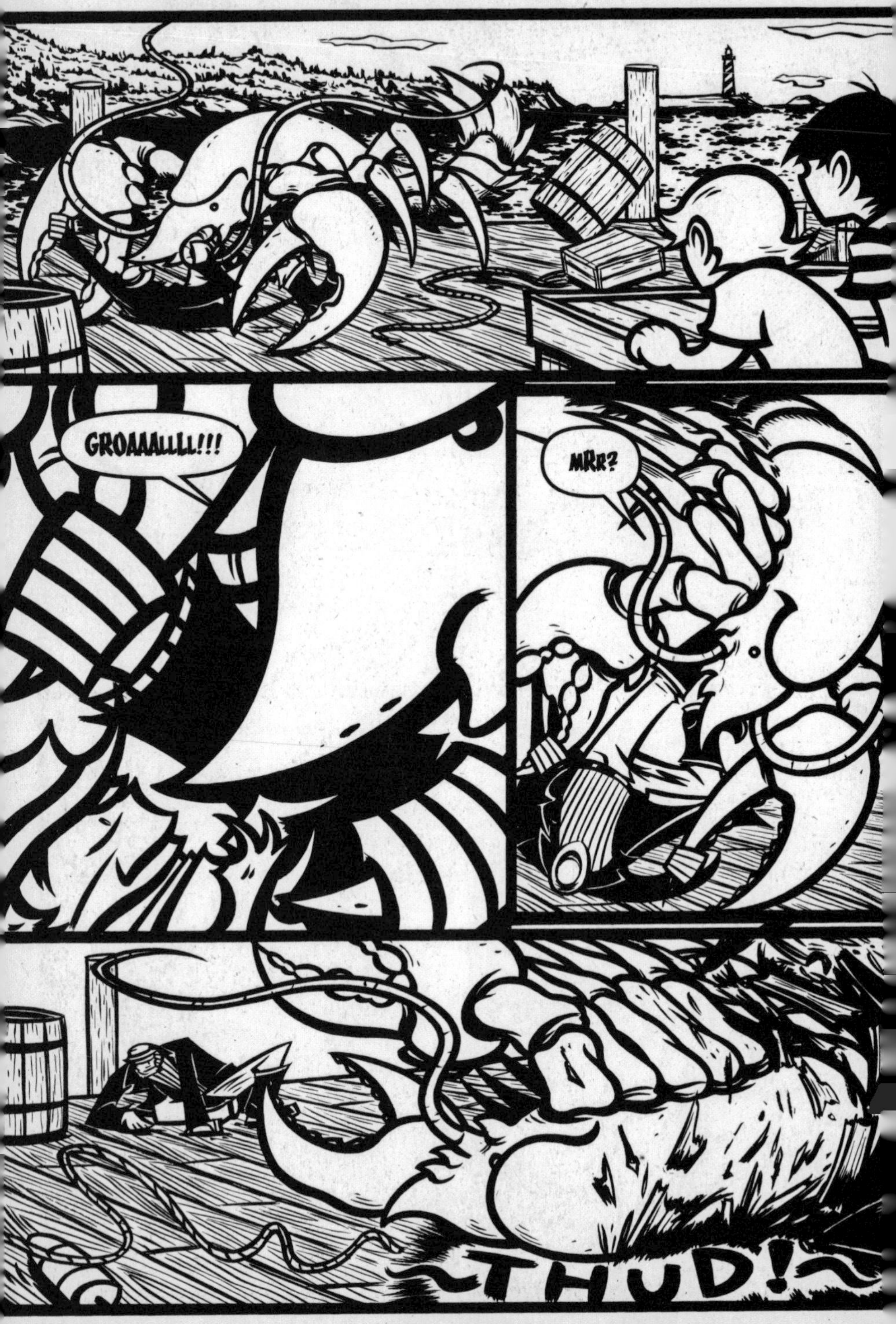
GROAAALLLL!!!
MRR?
~THUD!~

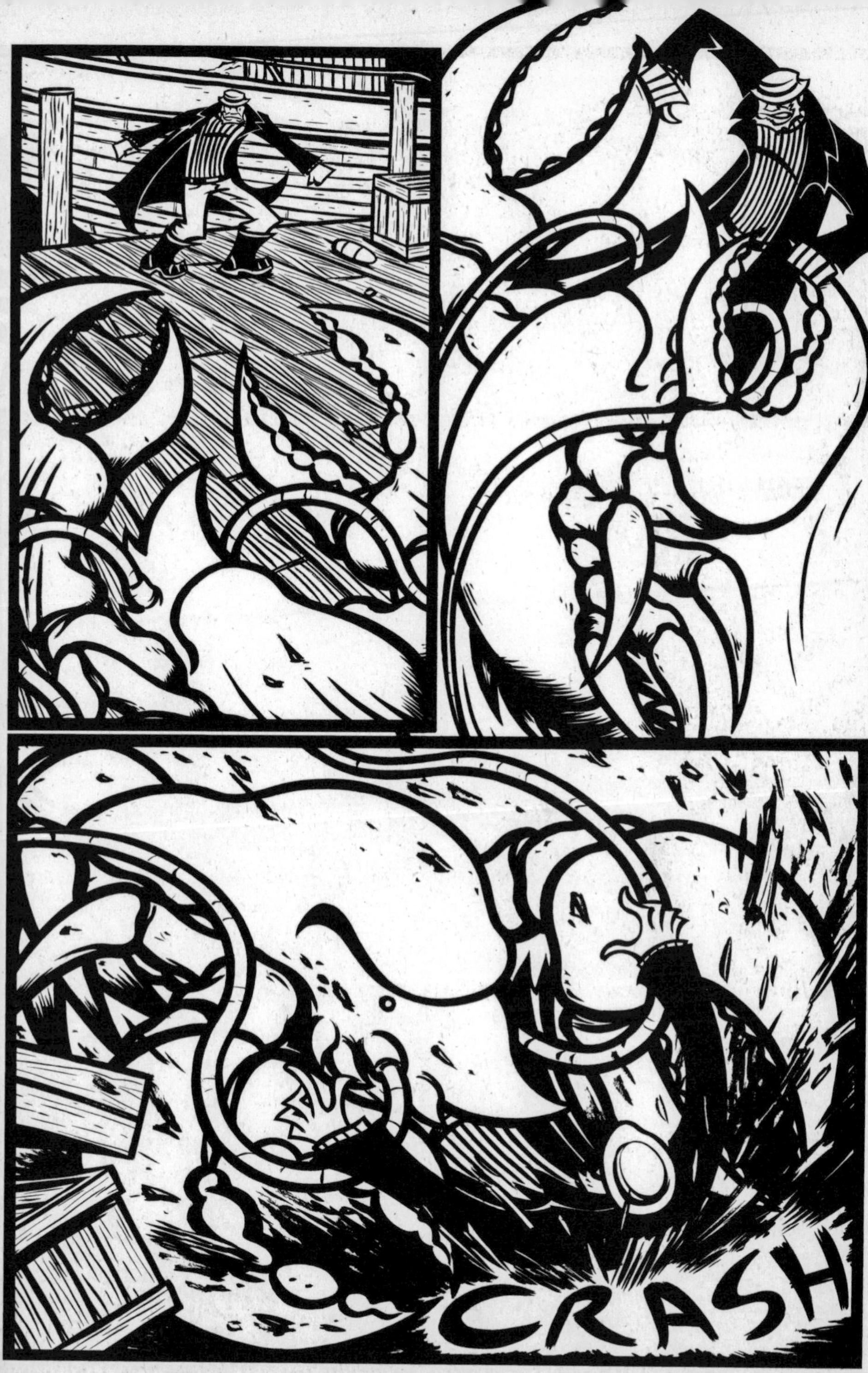
CRASH

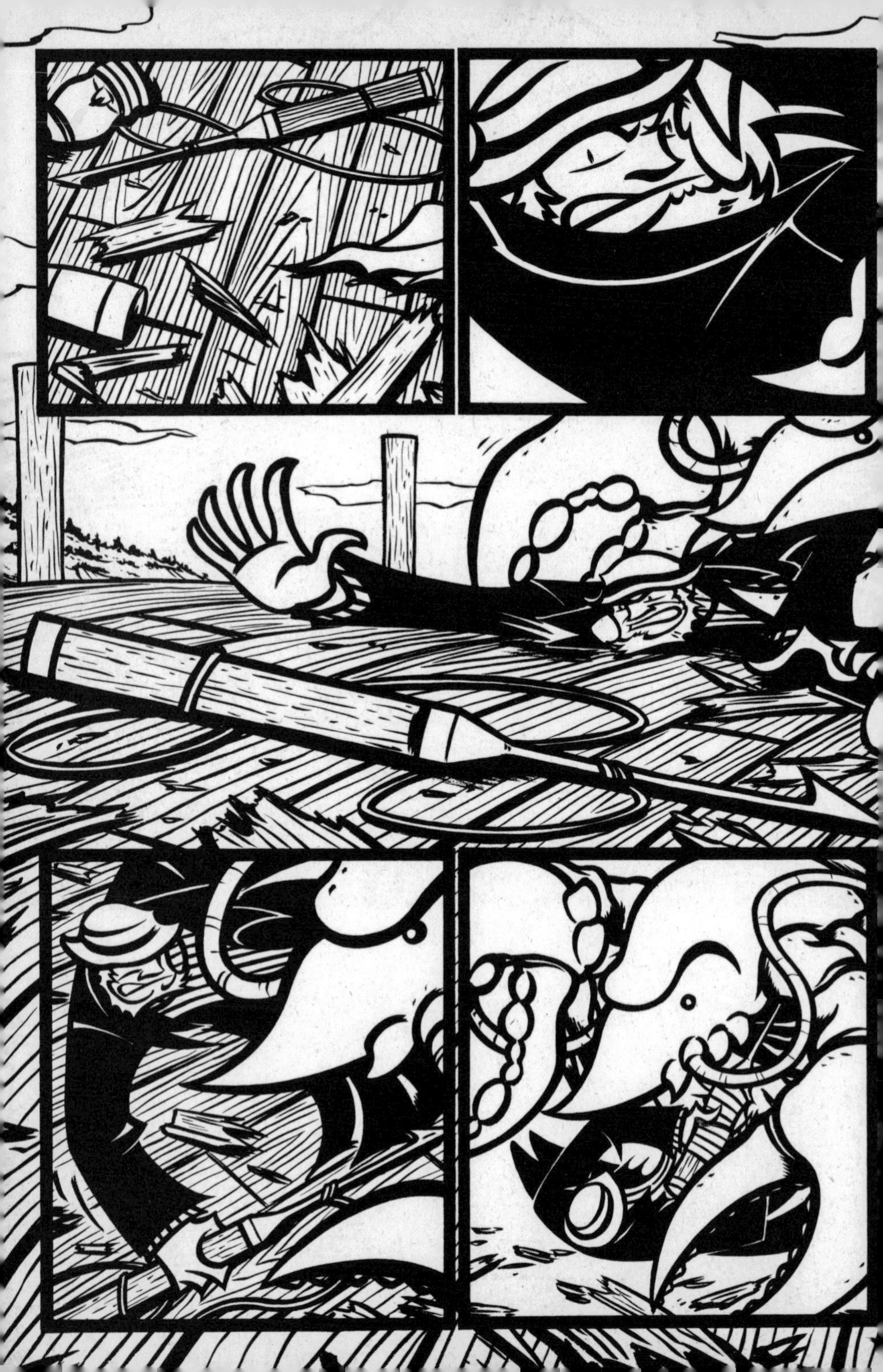

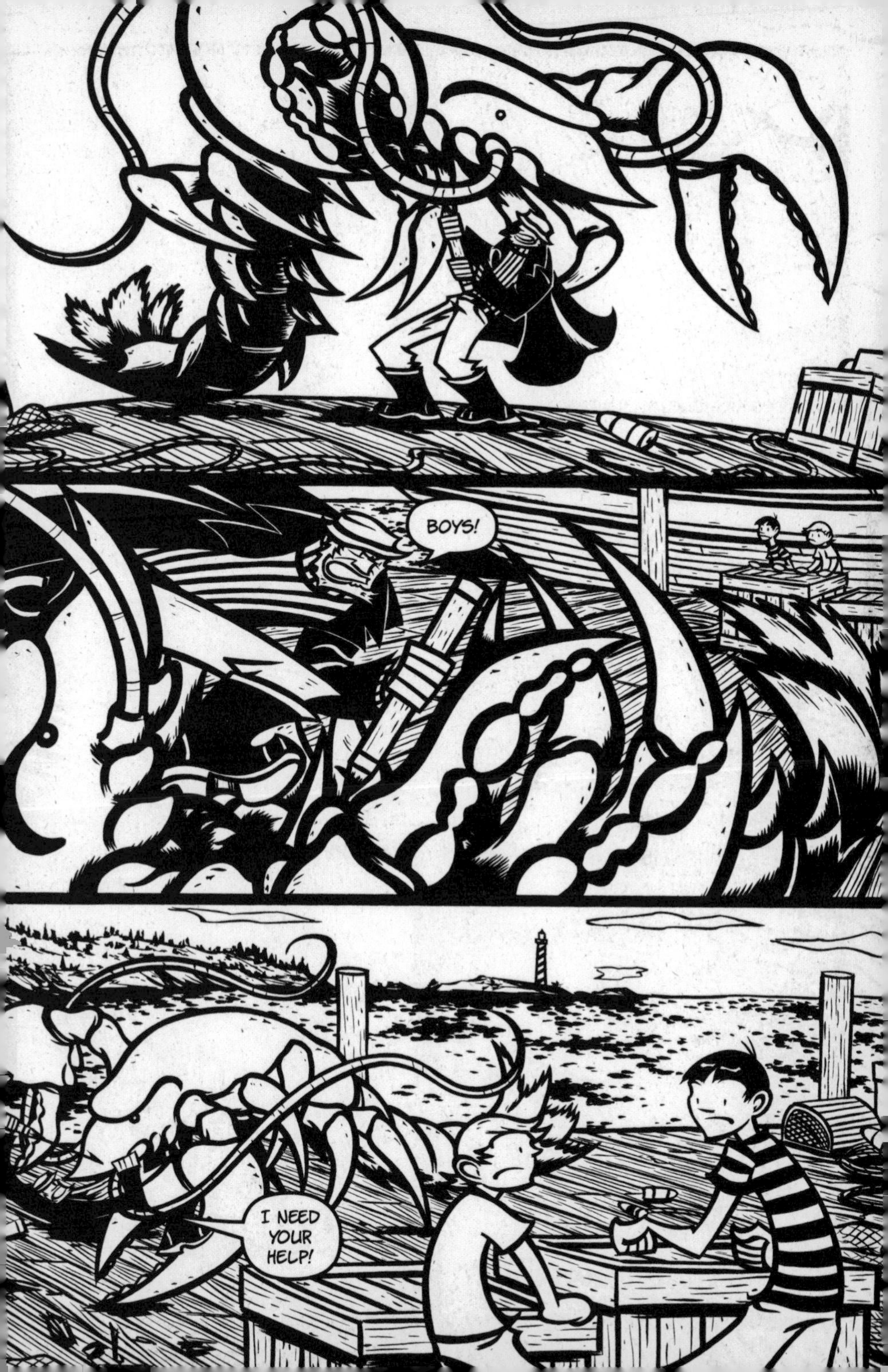
BOYS!
I NEED YOUR HELP!

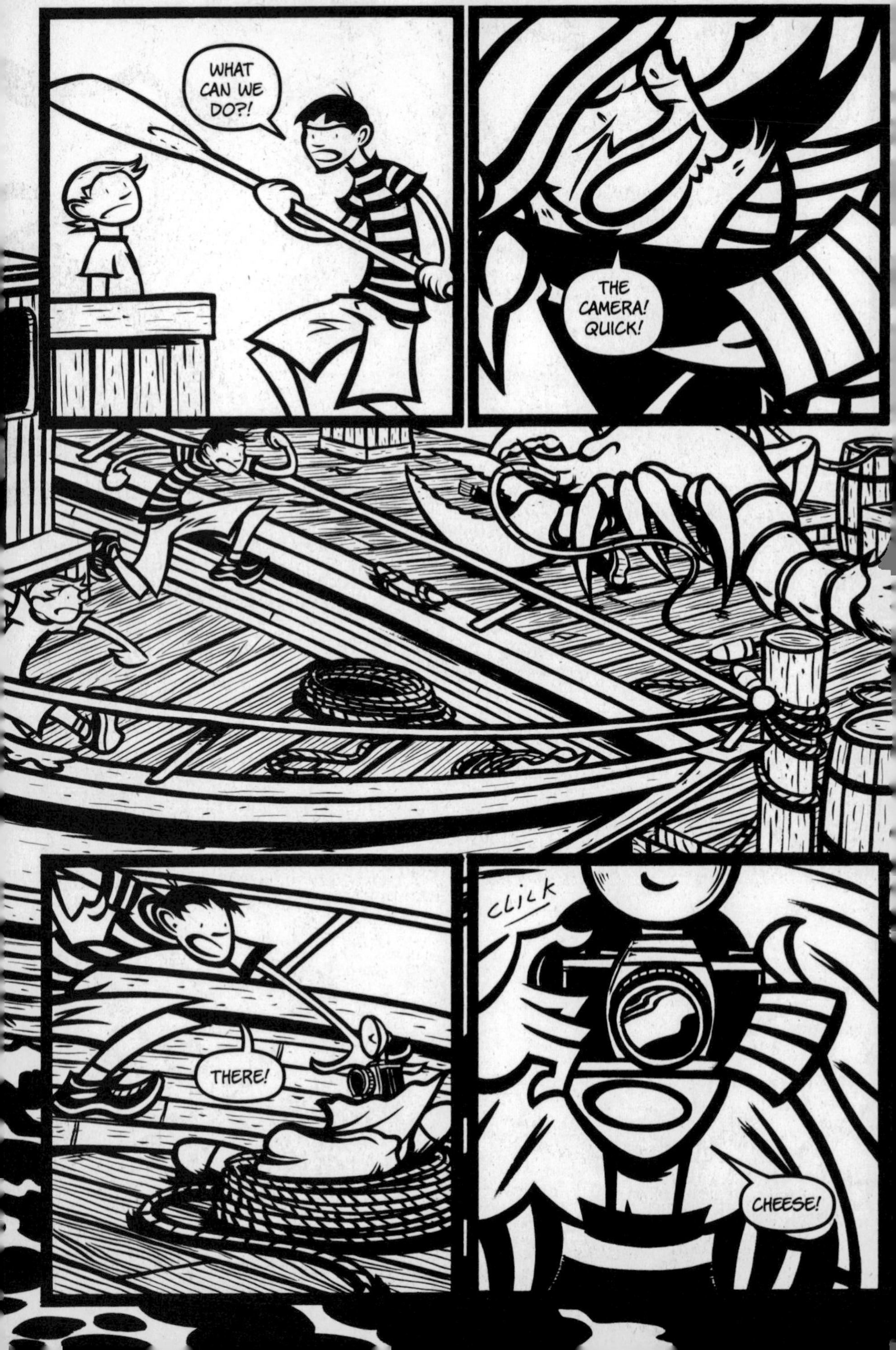
WHAT CAN WE DO?!
THE CAMERA! QUICK!
THERE!
CLICK
CHEESE!

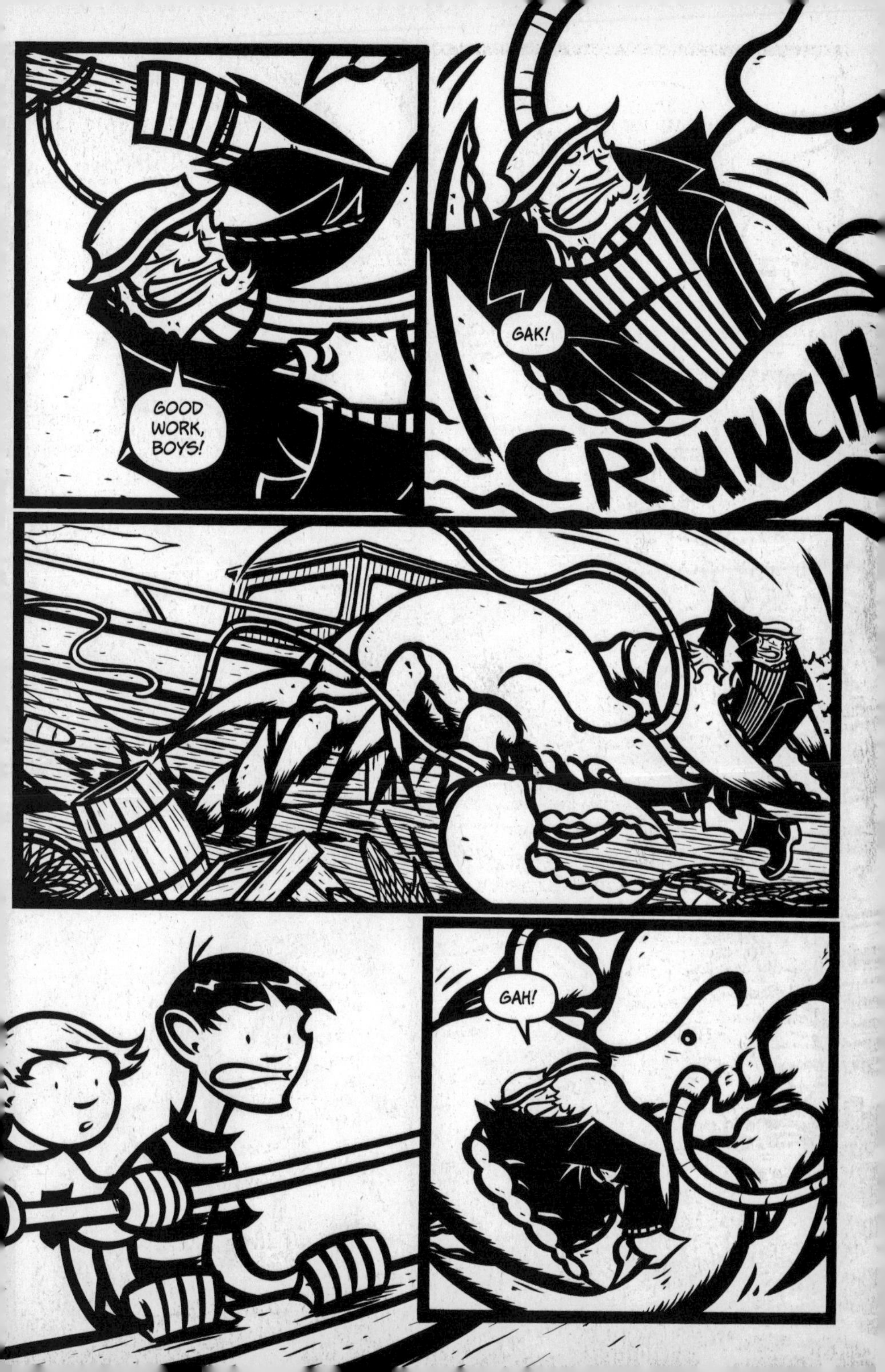
GOOD WORK, BOYS!
GAK!
CRUNCH
GAH!

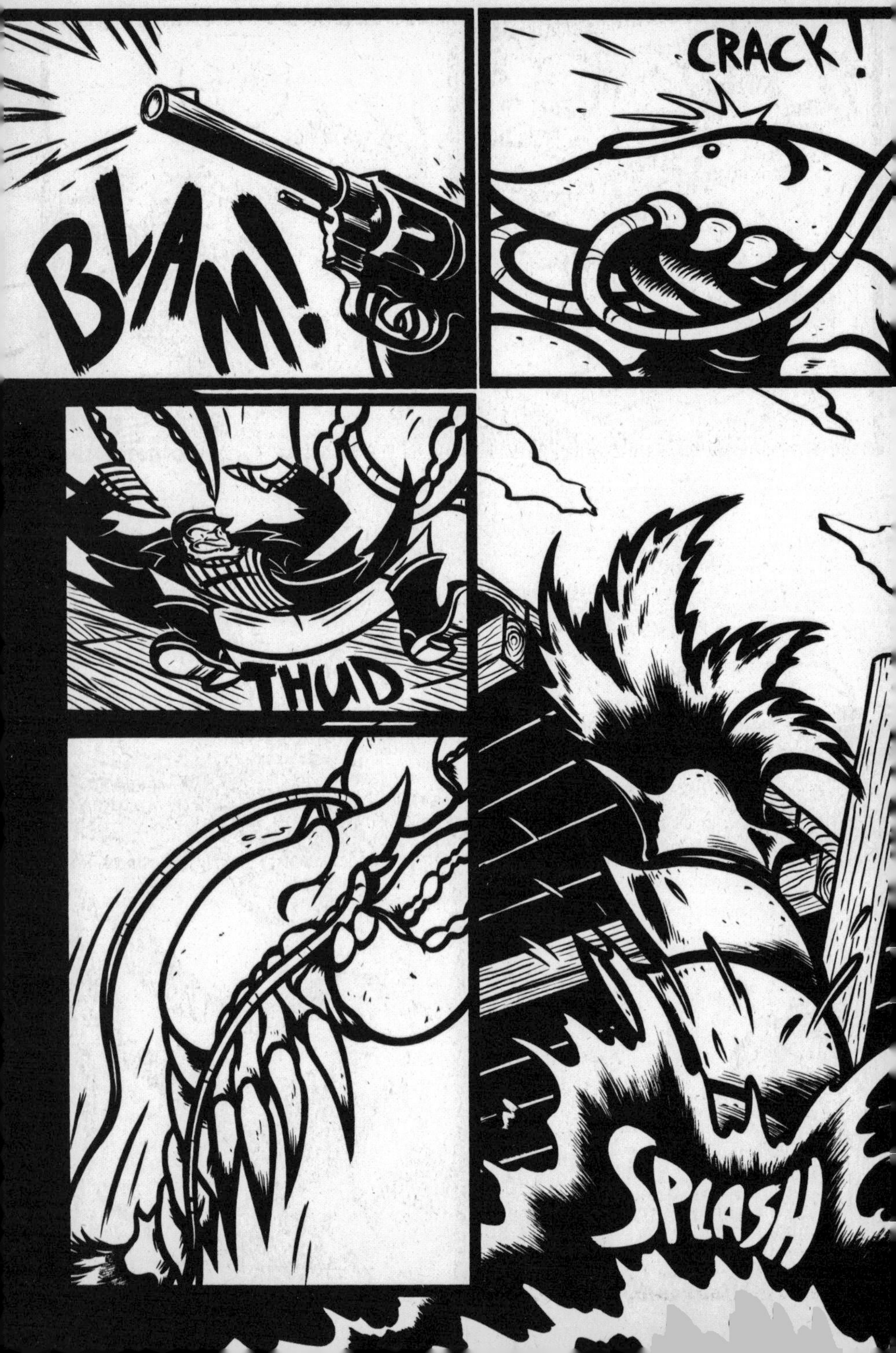
BLAM!
CRACK!
THUD
SPLASH

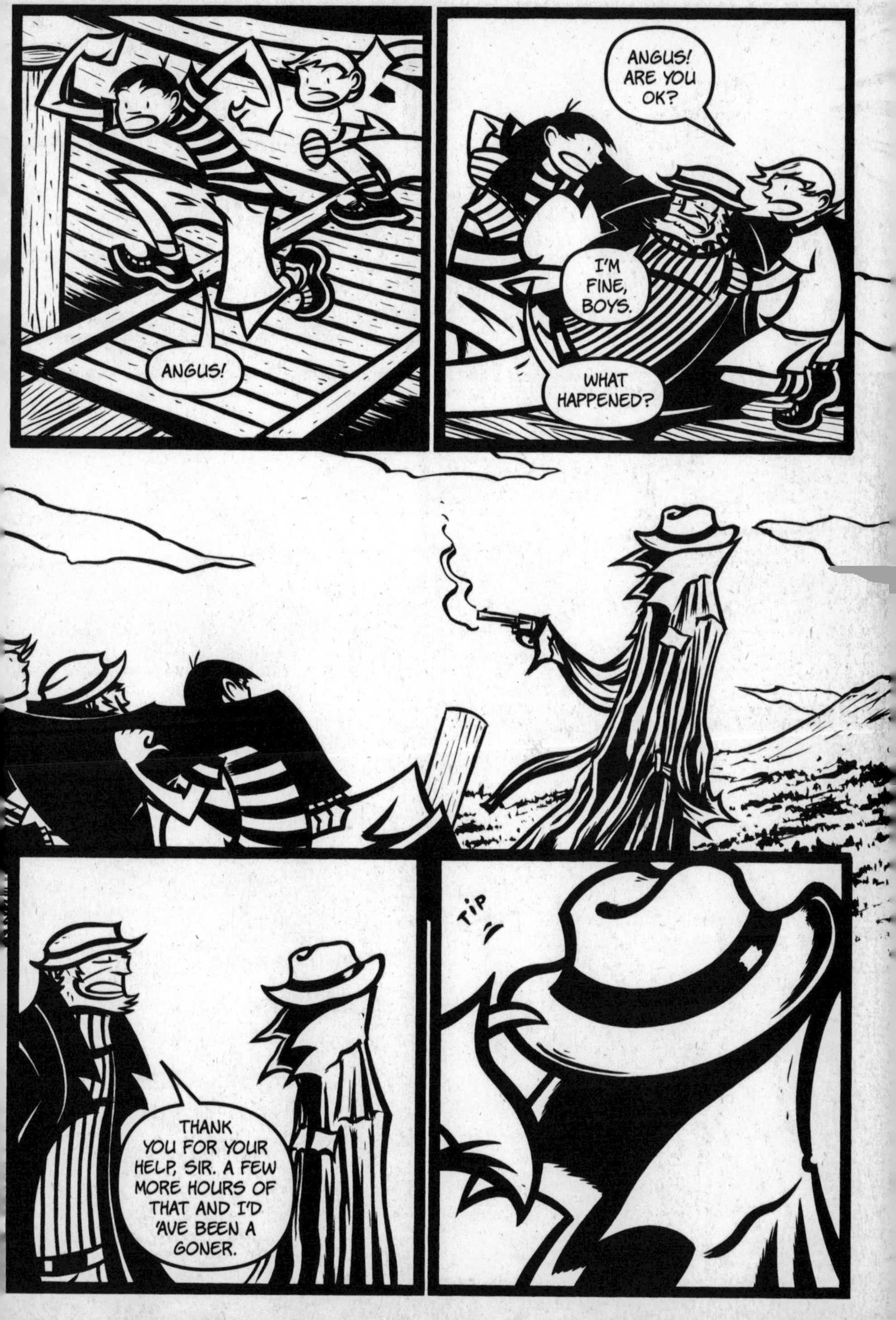
ANGUS!
ANGUS! ARE YOU OK?
I'M FINE, BOYS.
WHAT HAPPENED?
THANK YOU FOR YOUR HELP, SIR. A FEW MORE HOURS OF THAT AND I'D 'AVE BEEN A GONER.
TIP

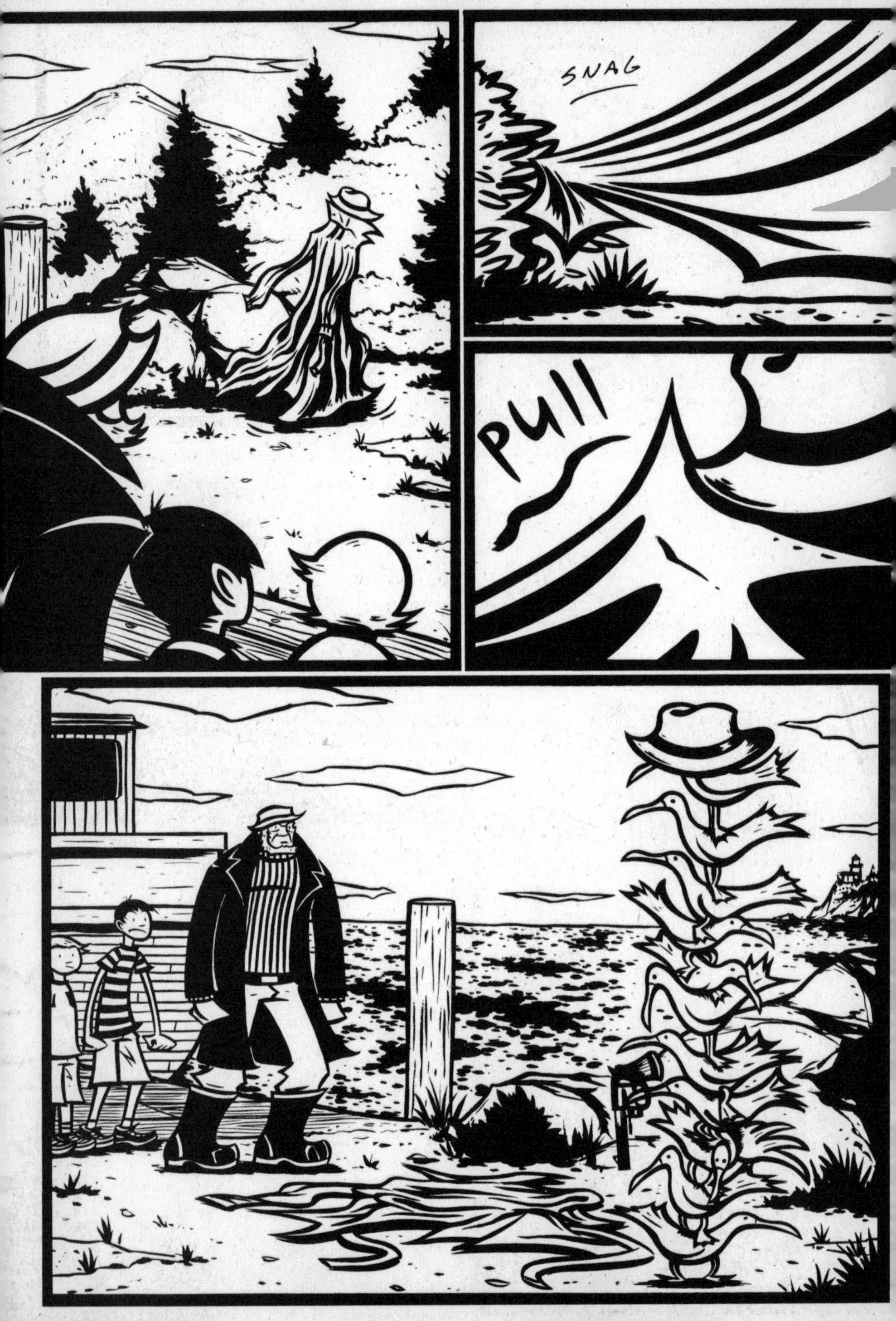
SNAG
PULL

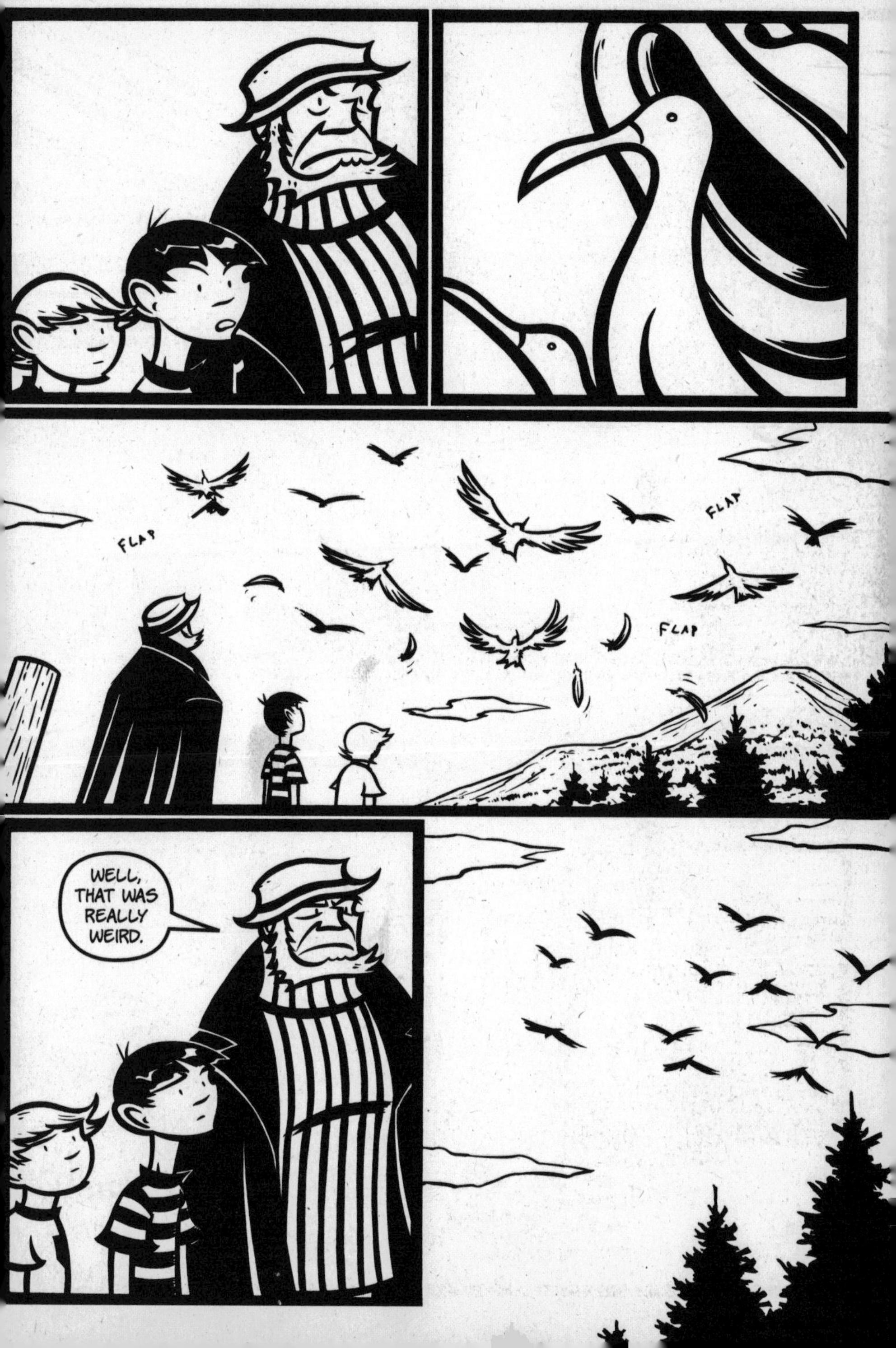
FLAP
FLAP
FLAP
WELL, THAT WAS REALLY WEIRD.

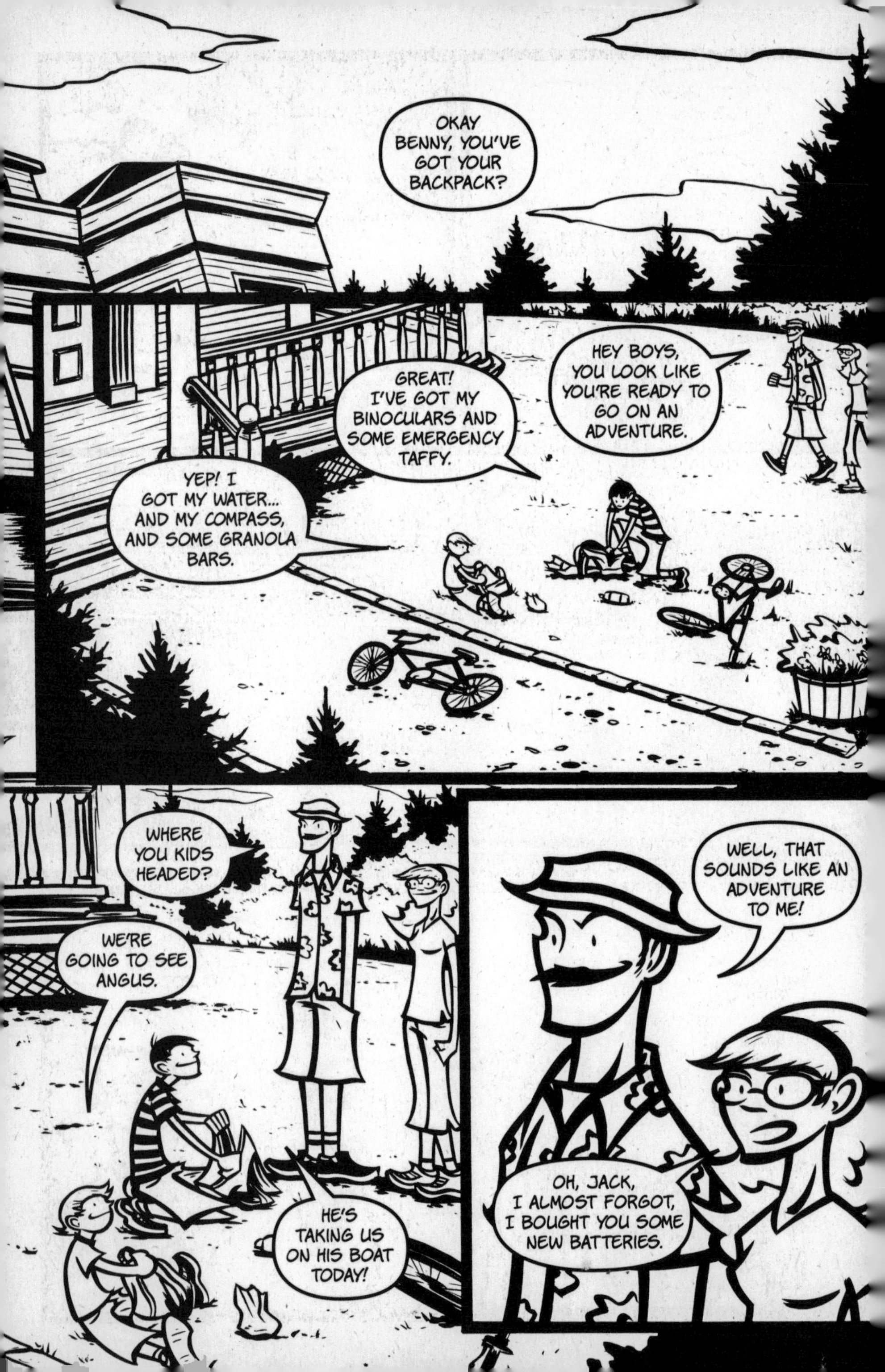

OKAY BENNY, YOU'VE GOT YOUR BACKPACK?
YEP! I GOT MY WATER... AND MY COMPASS, AND SOME GRANOLA BARS.
GREAT! I'VE GOT MY BINOCULARS AND SOME EMERGENCY TAFFY.
HEY BOYS, YOU LOOK LIKE YOU'RE READY TO GO ON AN ADVENTURE.
WHERE YOU KIDS HEADED?
WE'RE GOING TO SEE ANGUS.
HE'S TAKING US ON HIS BOAT TODAY!
WELL, THAT SOUNDS LIKE AN ADVENTURE TO ME!
OH, JACK, I ALMOST FORGOT, I BOUGHT YOU SOME NEW BATTERIES.

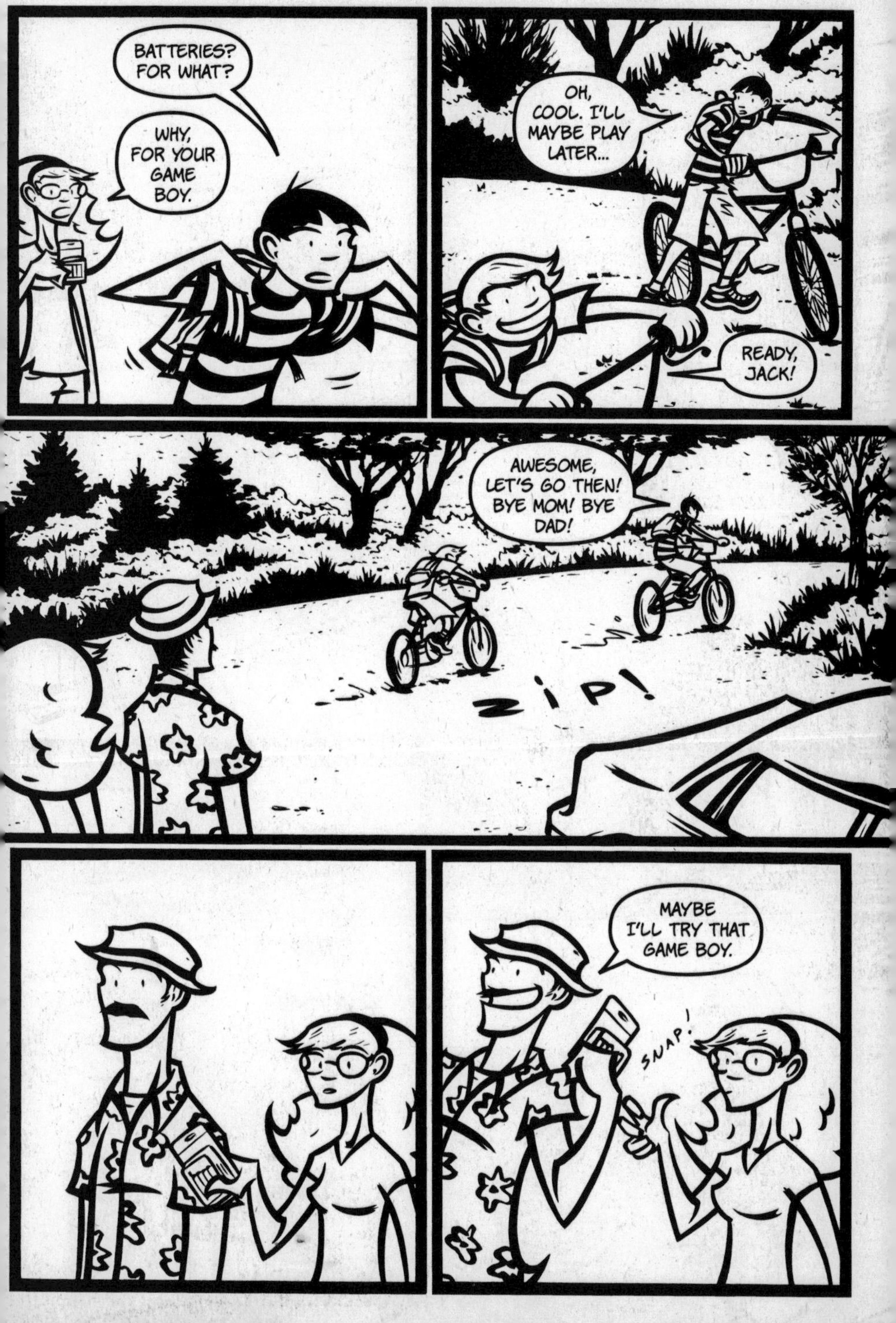
BATTERIES? FOR WHAT?
WHY, FOR YOUR GAME BOY.
OH, COOL. I'LL MAYBE PLAY LATER...
READY, JACK!
AWESOME, LET'S GO THEN! BYE MOM! BYE DAD!
ZIP!
MAYBE I'LL TRY THAT GAME BOY.
SNAP!

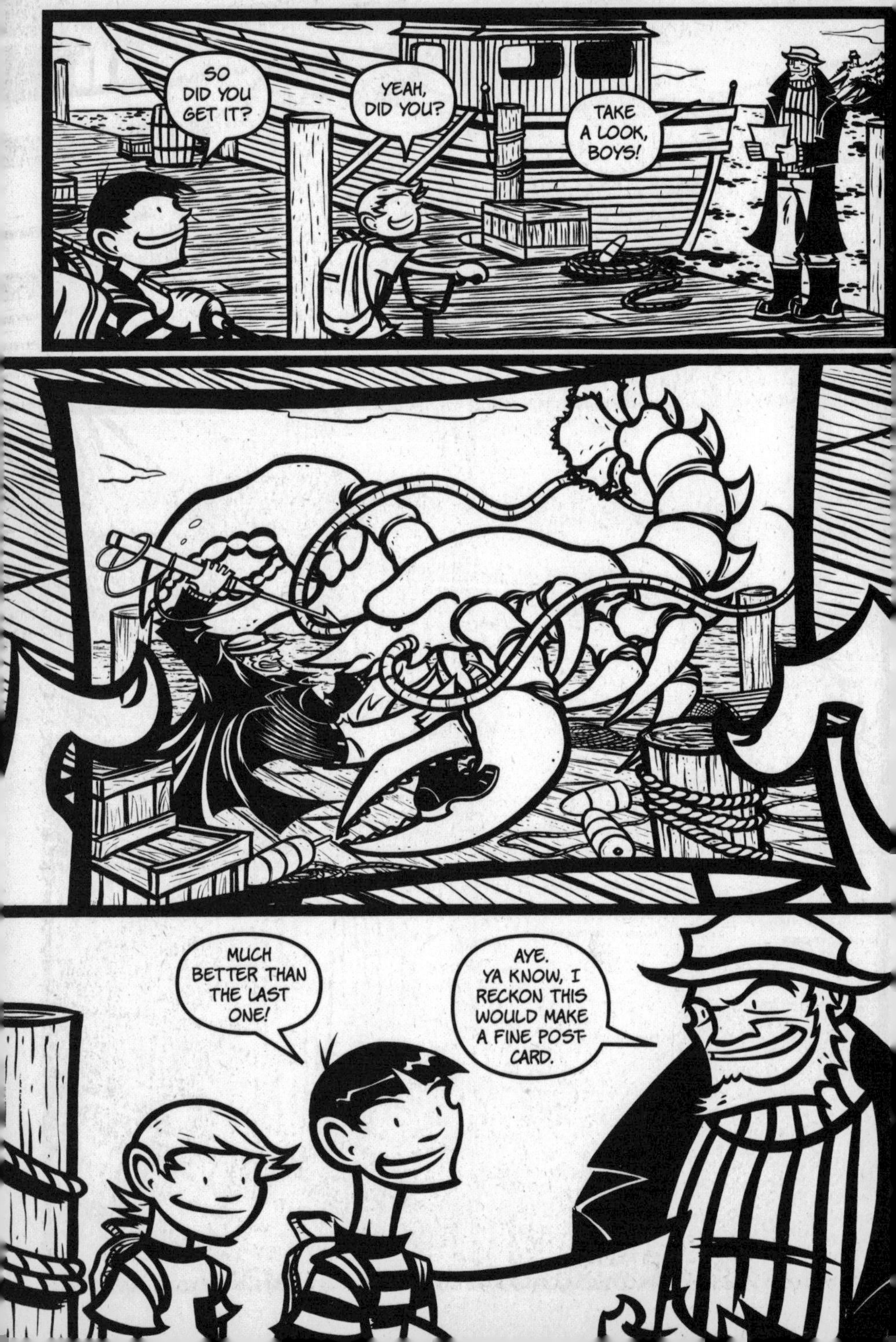
SO DID YOU GET IT?
YEAH, DID YOU?
TAKE A LOOK, BOYS!
MUCH BETTER THAN THE LAST ONE!
AYE. YA KNOW, I RECKON THIS WOULD MAKE A FINE POST CARD.

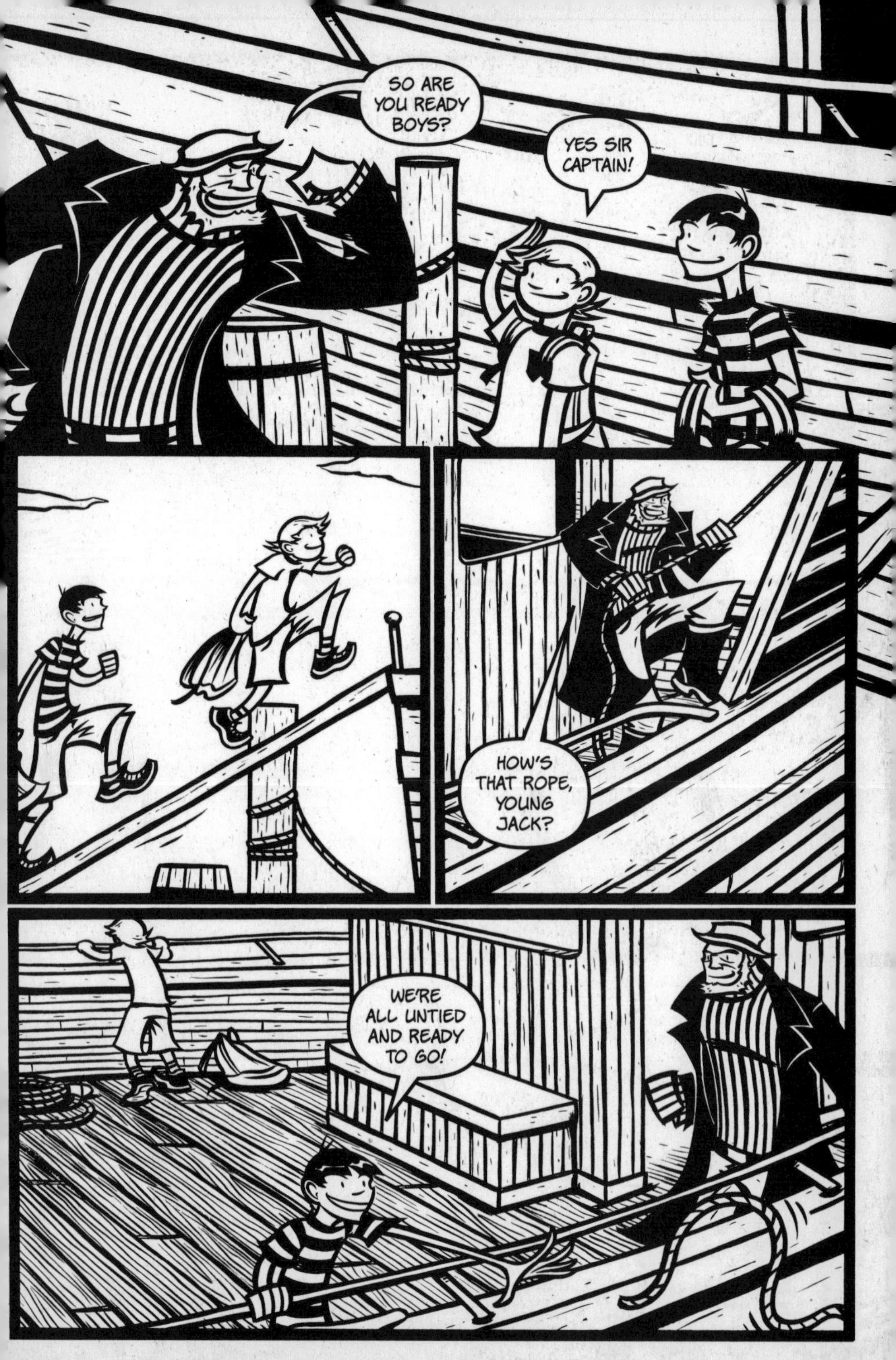
SO ARE YOU READY BOYS?
YES SIR CAPTAIN!
HOW'S THAT ROPE, YOUNG JACK?
WE'RE ALL UNTIED AND READY TO GO!

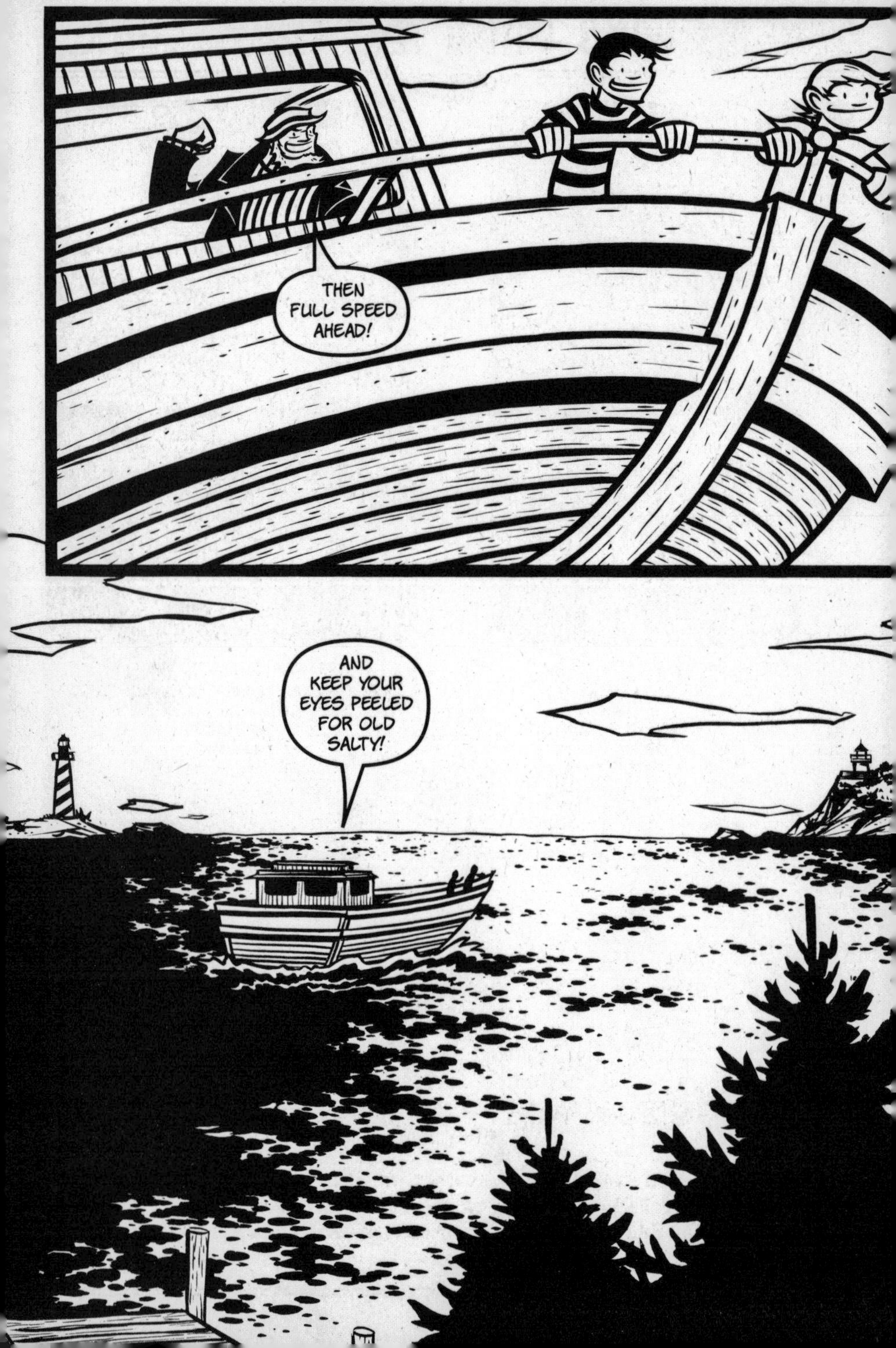
THEN FULL SPEED AHEAD!
AND KEEP YOUR EYES PEELED FOR OLD SALTY!

OTHER BOOKS FROM MATTHEW LOUX...

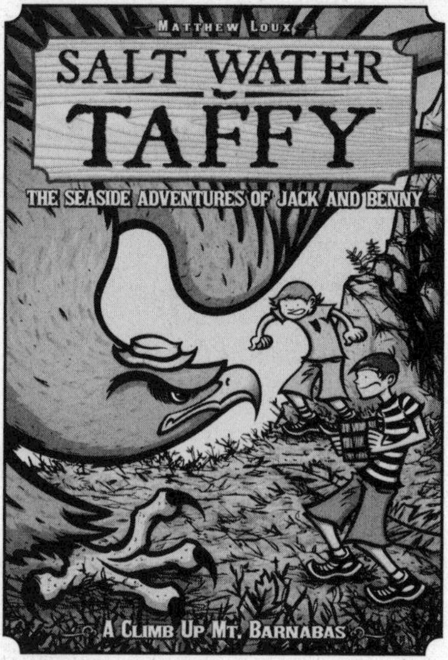
MATTHEW LOUX
SALT WATER TAFFY
THE SEASIDE ADVENTURES OF JACK AND BENNY
A CLIMB UP MT. BARNABAS

SALT WATER TAFFY™ VOL. 2:
"A CLIMB UP MT. BARNABAS"
written & illustrated by
Matthew Loux
96 pages • $5.99 US
ISBN: 978-1-934964-03-3

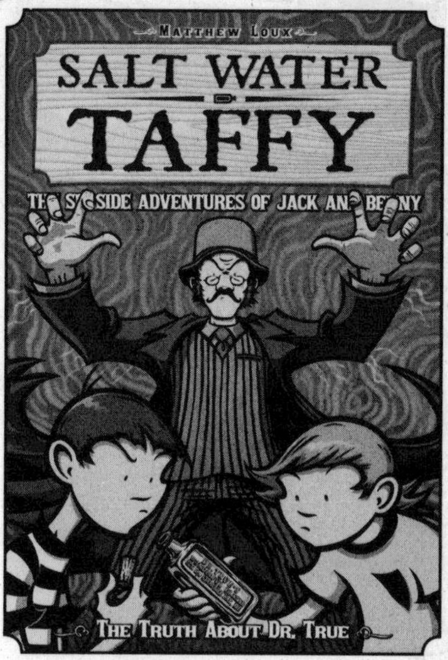
MATTHEW LOUX
SALT WATER TAFFY
THE TRUTH ABOUT DR. TRUE

SALT WATER TAFFY™ VOL. 3:
"THE TRUTH ABOUT DOCTOR TRUE"
written & illustrated by
Matthew Loux
96 pages • $5.99 US
ISBN: 978-1-934964-04-0

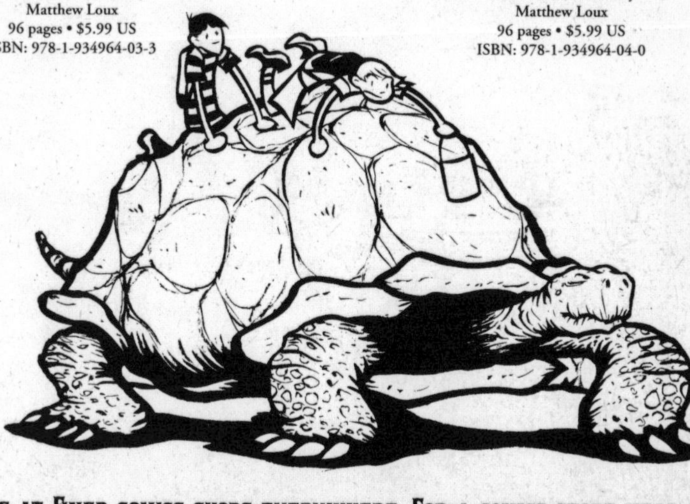

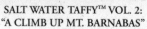

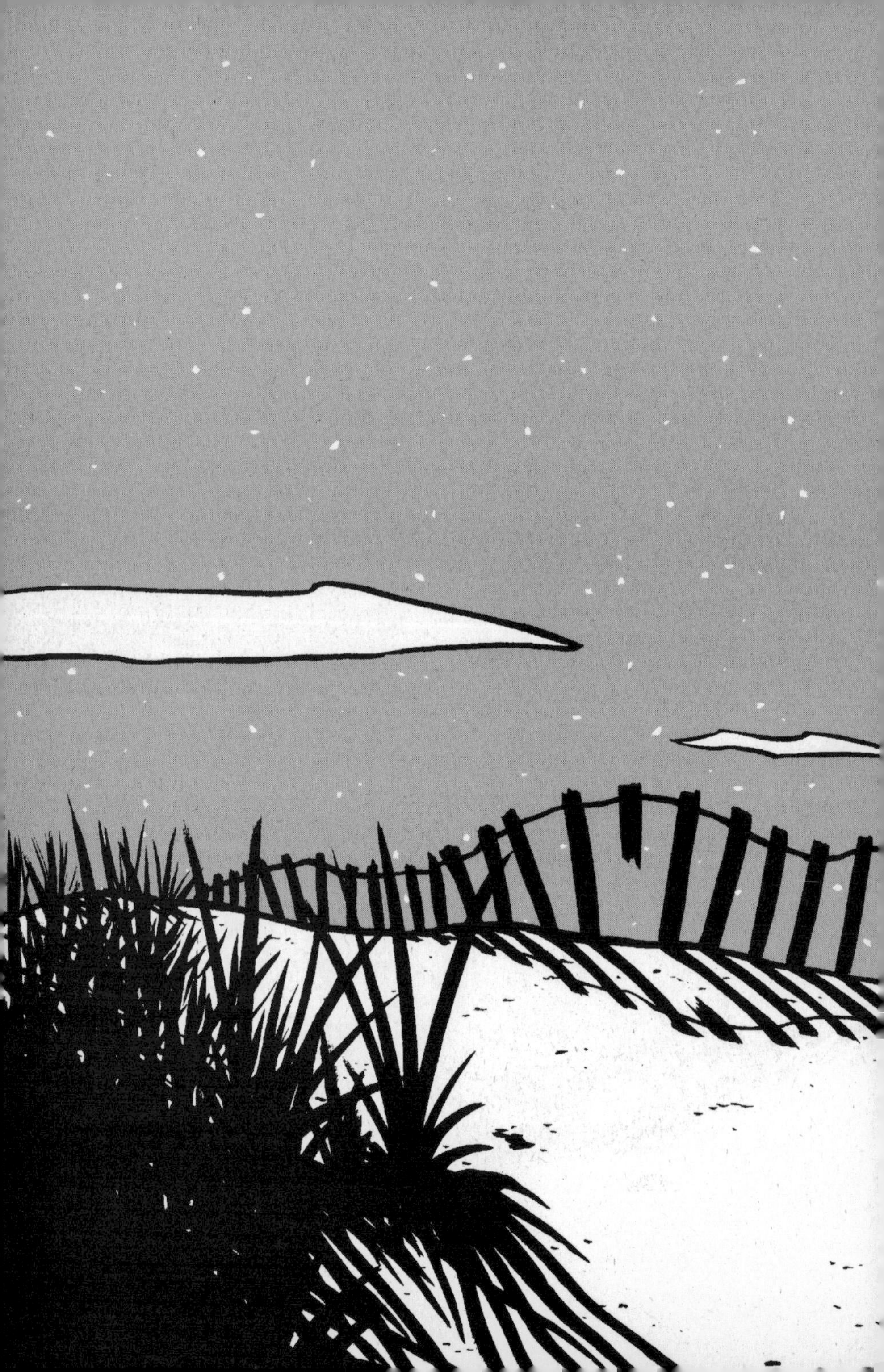

Matthew Loux grew up in eastern Connecticut and spent many a vacation along the New England coastline. He attended the School of Visual Arts in New York City and currently resides in Brooklyn.

actionmatt.com

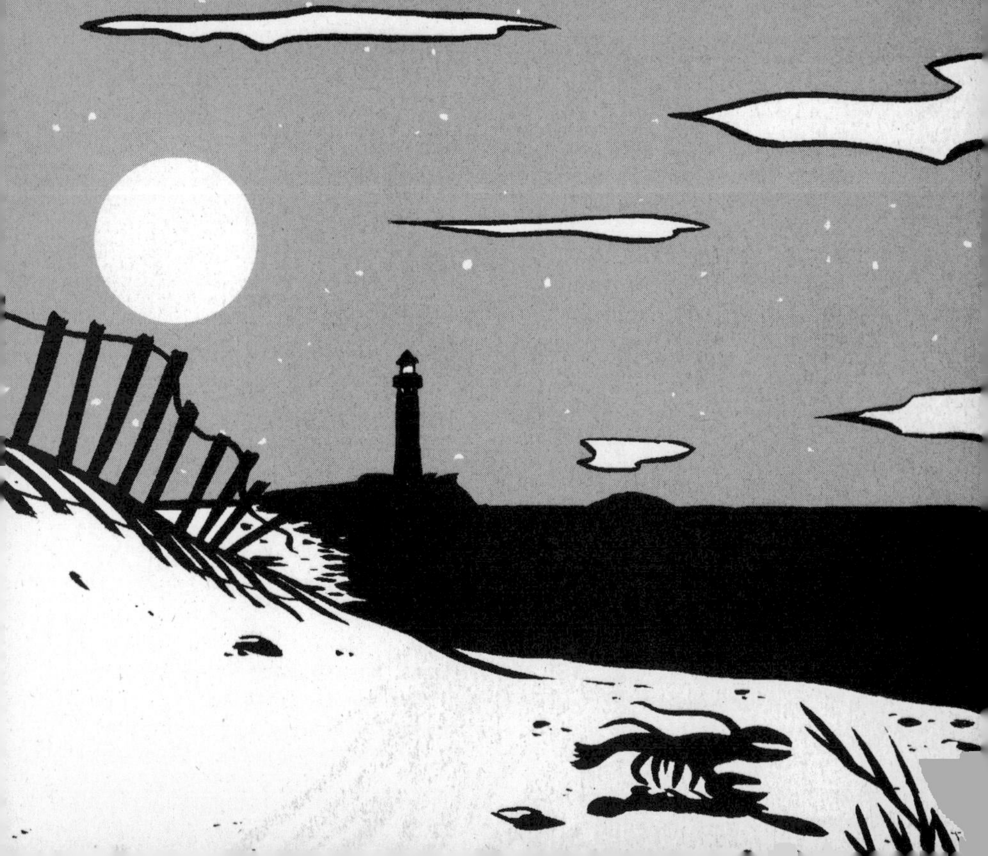

OTHER BOOKS FROM MATTHEW LOUX...

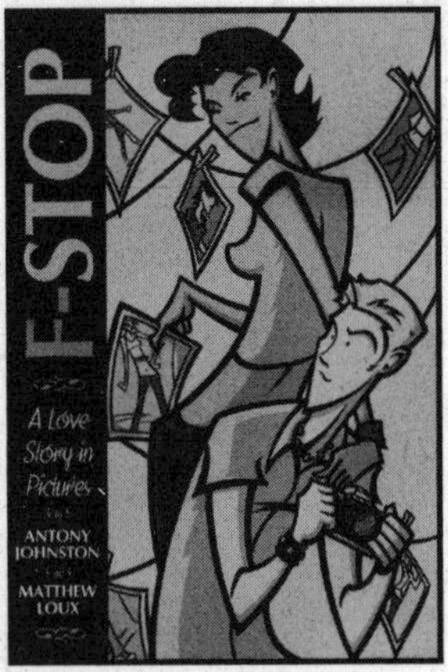
F-STOP
A Love Story in Pictures
ANTONY JOHNSTON
MATTHEW LOUX

F-STOP™
Written by Antony Johnston
Illustrated by Matthew Loux
168 pages • $14.95
ISBN: 978-1-932664-09-6

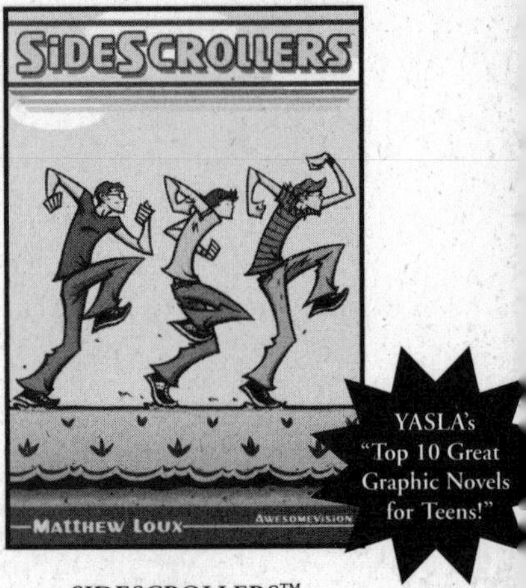
SIDESCROLLERS
MATTHEW LOUX
AWESOMEVISION
YASLA's "Top 10 Great Graphic Novels for Teens!"

SIDESCROLLERS™
Written & illustrated by
Matthew Loux
216 pages • $11.99 US
ISBN: 978-1-932664-50-8

OTHER BOOKS FROM ONI PRESS...

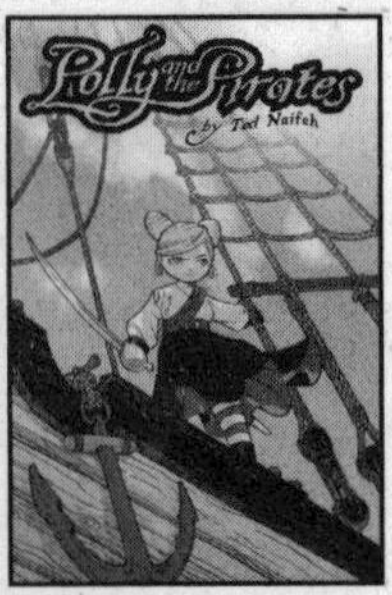
Polly and the Pirates
by Ted Naifeh

POLLY & THE PIRATES™
VOL. 1
Written & illustrated by
Ted Naifeh
176 pages • $11.95 US
ISBN: 978-1-932664-46-1

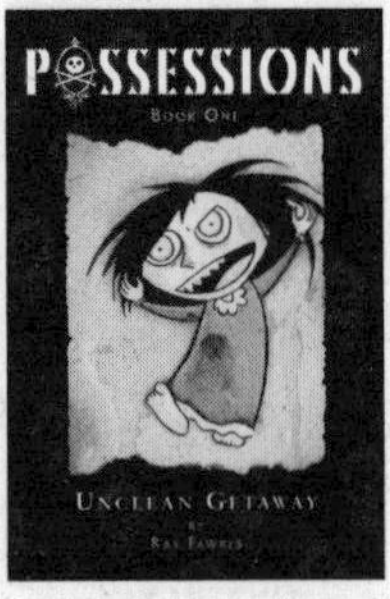
POSSESSIONS
BOOK ONE
UNCLEAN GETAWAY

POSSESSIONS ™
VOL. 1 UNCLEAN GETAWAY
Written & illustrated by
Ray Fawkes
88 pages • $5.99 US
ISBN: 978-1-934964-36-1

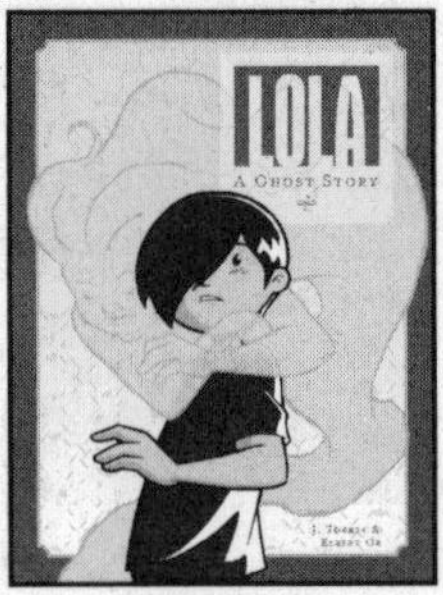
LOLA
A GHOST STORY

LOLA™
A GHOST STORY
Written by J. Torres
illustrated by Elbert Or
112 pages • $14.95 US
ISBN: 978-1-934964-33-0

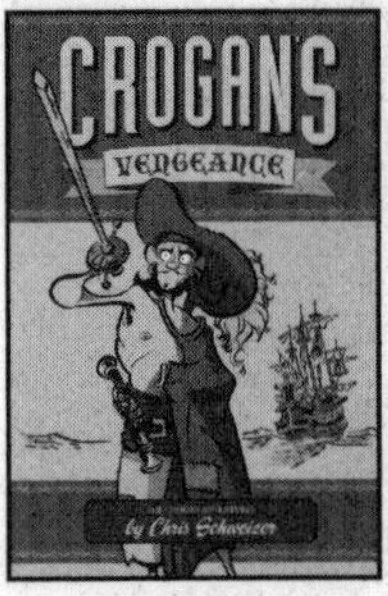
CROGANS
VENGEANCE
by Chris Schweizer

CROGAN'S VENGEANCE
Written & illustrated by
Chris Schweizer
Hardcover
192 pages • $14.99 US
ISBN: 978-1-934964-06-4

AVAILABLE AT FINER COMICS SHOPS EVERYWHERE. FOR A COMICS STORE NEAR YOU, CALL 1-888-COMIC-BOOK OR VISIT WWW.COMICSHOPS.US.

FOR MORE ONI PRESS TITLES AND INFORMATION VISIT WWW.ONIPRESS.COM.